DRAMA IN THE DESERT

The Sights and Sounds of Burning Man

Based on the images of Holly Kreuter

A Raised Barn Press Production

Producer: Holly Kreuter

Book Designer: Lisa Hoffman

Poetry Editors: M. Mara-Ann, Travis Ortiz

Prose Editors: Elinor Mills Abreu, Chris Taylor, Daniel Terdiman

Drama in the Desert Copyright 2002
By Raised Barn Press
San Francisco, CA

Images © Holly Kreuter except where noted
Poetry and prose © individual artists listed

This is the first in a series of Sight and Sound projects by Raised Barn Press

For more information on this and
upcoming projects, please visit:
www.raisedbarnpress.com

To view the *Drama in the Desert* DVD you will need a player that is capable of playing NTSC encoded discs. The disc itself is region-free.

The *Drama in the Desert* soundtrack is also available on audio CD. Visit our website for more information.
www.desertdrama.com

Printed in Singapore

ISBN 0-9721789-0-2

Preface

By Holly Kreuter

We are not artists who have built large sculptures on the playa. Some of us have formed small Theme Camps and shared simple things with the community. But mainly, we go to Burning Man each year to become inspired. We leave with new friends and the inspiration and energy we receive from the rest of Black Rock City, then we come home and apply it to our daily lives, our careers and our passions.

Drama in the Desert is our offering to those who give so much of themselves for several months leading up to and at Burning Man itself. Many of our skills come in different forms than are easily shown in the desert, and we have found through this project ways to express our gratitude to the community, as well as ways to reflect what we've seen and absorbed from participants' selfless labor.

When we began *Drama in the Desert* 14 months ago, over half the team was unemployed. We had just watched the Bay Area's technology boom go bust. We wanted to step back in time, to jump-start the creative lives we had led before the gold rush of Internet start-ups had consumed us. We began such an ambitious project in part because we wanted to stick with it, to stay focused on something other than the dismal economic forecast that dominated coffee shop conversations. Since our first meeting, the team has doubled in size, unemployment among team members has decreased and we have accomplished much more than we set out to do. It took 19 production people and 5 business types to make it happen, along with 40 writing contributors and 12 video contributors for a total of 76 collaborators.

I began shooting photographs and collecting sound in 1997 with the intention of producing a documentary look at Burning Man. At the time, I envisioned it as a CD-ROM, maybe a video if it turned out to be a good piece of work. I didn't feel the collection of images was complete until 2000, when I decided a soft-cover book would be the best media. I liked the idea of returning to paper after the digital mania had subsided. It soon became a book with a soundtrack, stepping up to a book with a CD-ROM, then solidified as a hard-cover book and DVD. Having surpassed an attempt to simply document Burning Man, what we present to you as the reader, viewer and listener is an attempt to create an experience. Hold onto your cowboy hats …

I woke up and rode my bike toward the thumping

Foreword by Dave Eggers

So go. Go with people you barely know. Pack lightly and go. Go and drive to Reno and on, and by the time you get to the site, shortly after that taxidermy place by the roadside and before the train tracks, your car will be tanned with dust, you will be tanned with dust, the black upholstery of your rental car — I recommend renting a car — will be tanned with dust, all the tapes in your rental car will have in them this incredibly fine dust, and you will be wearing funny hats. You and the people you barely know. So go. Go and set up your tent. Or go and wait to set up your tent until it's dark and you're in bad shape to set up your tent. It won't matter. Go and skip the tent the first night because it's hard to sleep that first night. Why sleep that first night? It's too hard. There are too many people dancing. There is a thumping that travels through the desert earth, and it will remind you that elsewhere people are dancing. Over the days you will be reminded often that people are always dancing somewhere. Somewhere people are naked and somewhere people are racing their bikes into a desert whose endlessness is both true and deceptive. So go if you like to race your bike, and if you like to dance or know that people are somewhere dancing. Go and don't overworry about the needs and ifs and how muches. You need not be a professional to come. You need not be a professional camper, or a professional arty person, or a professional naked person, or a professional fire-liker, or a professional drug-enthusiast. So go. Go and maybe even try — just an idea, definitely not a directive — to be there without any consumed enhancements. Just an idea. Many people go and use substances of one kind or another but I am here to say that this is not a prerequisite, not at all, and the debate, I offer, is open, as to the necessity of enhancement use, because, for instance: why go so far and have so many stimuli around you, so many things made and built, so many brilliant ideas standing there in the flat plain plane, only

to bend your senses to warp and muddy things further? If everyday reality requires sometimes for many some enhancement via this or that substance, then wouldn't this desert festival, searing in its intelligence, soaring in its beauty — daytime a dry flat desert make-do community at the end of the world; nighttime a bent, Lewis Carrollian, self-illuminated settlement of artist-engineers under stars and on the top of the moon, itself a 24-a-day natural hallucination — be enough without chemical enhancement? Again, just an idea, just a notion, and a go-to nod to those who have stayed away — I have spoken to you people and know why you think what you think — because there should be no reason to stay away, there are none with strong-beating hearts who would not find glory there. Glory there! Everyone likes glory. To eschew Burning Man is to eschew glory both natural and manmade. It is saying the Grand Canyon is ho-hum, that Antarctica is ho-hum, that Annapurna is for a certain kind of person but not for you. So go. Yes if you can, walk around nude in the mud baths, paint your friends or acquaintances with mud and leap from pond to pond, some ponds hotter than others, some smellier, some just absolutely stinking with sulfur, and then float while holding onto the reeds surrounding the pools, and float for an hour there, fall into a shallow sleep there and dream of trucks with large elephant trunks who can talk and do so in terrific East-Indian accents. Then wake up and notice the population of the pond has doubled. It will be full. Yes there will be so many naked people, so many painted naked people. And always at

Burning Man the naked men on bicycles. Why so many naked men on bicycles? All of the naked men on bicycles have to be 40 years old and bearded. See them and see the people clothed while biking, and notice how strange it soon becomes to see people biking clothed, and notice the many people walking from and to their campers. They are thinking of things to make you think. Everyone is thinking, thinking — thinking in a general and generous way but thinking, thinking. Can you believe the thinking? Can you see this as a gigantic biennial, ten times the size of even Documenta, with everything out there, standing against a plain blue sky met by a plain white cracked earth? Yes there are: a group of people who will trade poems for beer, and on the last night they will throw their poems onto the fire, which will seem both tragic and almost redundant. This all will be: serious, in its way. This will be: engineered, by engineers, planned, by planners, without being over-engineered or over-planned. It will be about ease, about an unobtrusive sense of order, order rendered by small stakes and on them small red flags, indicating roads just-made and on the ground: the earth will be cracked precisely like cracked earth is supposed to be. There will be: in many encampments, many small doorways you can duck into and which lead into hundreds of options, from the profane to the sacred and back again. People will be eating strange food and normal food and young people will be giving massages to old people. The train: will come once a night. It will be a dark train. There will be no lights on the train. But come. But if you do come, I beg you to come wanting to be there. The success of Burning Man — and by that I mean its ability to conjure and sustain an interlocking and inclusive lattice connecting its participants, a lattice receiving, giving back and maintaining a spirit of simply overwhelming goodwill — for that is, besides the startling clarity of the desert sky and the heaving breathing animate artwork below, what makes Burning Man Burning Man — depends on the shared diving-in and faith (in one another) of every last naked or un-naked person present. One skeptic, one disgruntled person who has come to debunk, can and will infect

and erode the spirit of the place, will gnaw at and make weak the lattice, which is, like all lattices, fragile like the bones of the smallest of birds. So come but come wanting to be there. Because Burning Man, I shamelessly believe, is, despite its eccentricities, a microcosm of how all large groups of strangers can act when thrown together in a foreign, semi-forgiving and even hostile environment. The success of any group living together in situations of isolation or even centrality relies on the minute-to-minute decisions, made by every last person, to be generous. Generous in their eyes. Generous in their mouths, in their thoughts. Wanting others to enjoy themselves — and not feeling, as we all have occasionally done, that the happiness of others, however achieved or expressed, impedes or precludes our own personal happiness. Burning Man is like, in a weird way, a small Kansan town where everyone knows each other and wishes each other well, demonstrates every last ideal of community — and of course first and foremost that community demands the participation of all. So go if you would like to see, quite frankly and ever-truly, the best that people can do and the best people can be, in the clarity of their heads and the way they touch the forearms of their fellow people. You should do that while you're there — touch the forearms. Touch the forearms of the people dancing between 20-foot-tall speakers a mile from the closest tent, touch the forearms of those walking under the arches of the full-scale children's-book castle built in a week from steel and wire and clay and papier-mâché, touch the forearms of the people who come via plane and those who come via bus and those via rental car tan with dust, with people they barely know. Keep your eyes open and touch the forearms. Keep everything you have open and touch the forearms. 🔥

Introduction

by Larry Harvey

Seventeen years ago I founded Burning Man on a beach in San Francisco. This is frequently the first thing people ask me about. They want a myth. I was once incautious enough to tell a reporter that it corresponded to the anniversary of a broken love affair. That story has now circled the globe and been interpreted and reinterpreted as myths often are. I've heard that I was burning myself, that I was burning my ex-girlfriend, that I was burning my ex-girlfriend's new boyfriend. But none of these stories are true. They are factoids, myths in the modern sense of the word — distortions of the truth. And yet people keep asking me this question, and I think it is because they're looking for a myth in the older and more profound sense of this term. Myths are the souls of our actions. They're not about historic circumstance or personal contingency. We moderns think that if we add all of these things up we can explain what happens in the world. But myths are not about chains of causation or rational reasoning. They contemplate an unconditional reality. They tell us the essence of a thing resides in its first cause. That's what people ask for. That is the nature of the story that they need to hear.

So I will tell you that story. One day in 1986 I called a friend and said, "Let's build a man and burn him on the beach." I did this on an impulse. There was really nothing in my mind. Some passionate prompting, some immediate vision just had to be embodied in the world. Call it radical self-expression. I am. We built our man from scraps of wood, then called some friends and took it to the beach. We saturated it with gasoline and put a match to it, and within moments our numbers had doubled. People came running and instantly formed a semi-circle. I was holding my young son in my arms, and I remember looking at each face illuminated in the firelight. We are. And then, of course, there was the Man himself. We had built it two crucial feet taller than ourselves. Standing there against the limitless horizon of the broad Pacific, it seemed to belong to the ocean, to belong to the sky, to exist in a realm immeasurably beyond us. It formed a fireball, a second sun brought down to earth, this sudden, uncontrollable and completely spontaneous emission of energy. It is.

And when I look at Black Rock City today, I notice that its curving streets are like that semi-circle of people so many years ago on Baker Beach. Our city seems to reach out toward the Man, as if it would capture him, but can never quite possess this gift at its center. I am. We are. It is. What more is there to say except that I believe there is a way that all of us can be together. 🔥

— From an address at Cooper Union
New York City, April 25, 2002

Photograph by Gabe Kirchheimer, 2000

Dust rewarding. A reverent cycle in giving and the beginning celebration of peaceful gratitude. Rendering within the singular and upon a relationship to the community.

Friendly understandings in a mutual truth and the inexplicable abundance of spontaneous desire. A pure wealth radiant throughout immediate experience.

Imagination's chariot reveling in the likelihood of destiny. The dynamism of sight angled carefully along the momentum of contemplative grace. An expanded flow within the possibilities of awareness.

Liberating transformation of opposites and the spinning evolutionary unity of a directed cycle. The adaptive mobility present among a timely spirit. Inevitability transferred at an intersection's resolve.

A fiery shape desiring expression through the potent exploration of joy and the timeless nature of passion. A liberating performance fusing creative metaphor and the limitlessness of vitality. The magnificent journey emanating possibility.

Unifying light and dark. An intimate vision of harmony entwined with purpose and the complex alchemy of air, fire, water, earth and spirit. A universal locus in the duty of inspiration.

Focused community inspired through purposeful connection and resonant unity. The sensitive unveiling of responsibility and the individual. Their respective care.

An unobstructed channel of belief and the infinite wisdom of ritual. Sacred understandings of insight among elemental mysteries. The teacher as student and the infinite form of reciprocity.

Compassionate legacy. The grounded depth of emotional elegance. An evolutionary birthright in the cycle of tides and an ancient guardian firmly anchoring beginning and presence. Wise counselor of truth.

The transcendent complement mirroring generosity and a meditative integration. A resolute empathy in unified wholeness. The perfect correspondence between intimacy and consummate integrity.

Respectful fulfillment. Ageless cooperation. The vehicle of fate.

Dawn purifies. Regenerative beginnings through the sacred melding of mind and the creative forces of fire and wind. An opportunity igniting the precious aspects of force and the nurturing embrace of light. A spark and opportunity. Welcome!

M. Mara-Ann

When I found myself with my hands on the wagon wheel steering our faithful ol' school bus, heading down Highway 34 toward the Black Rock playa, it was like going back to sleep and picking up a dream where I had left off. This was August 1st, and my survey crew and I were heading out to the site with back-to-school excitement: new clothes, new books and a freshly washed chalkboard. Today we would be spotting the first flags that would eventually determine the sculpture that is Black Rock City.

Midsummer weather on the high desert is anything but typical, but it does wear a standard face that it sometimes holds for weeks. Hot and dry, a powerful sun set way high in a boundless cloudless sky, all of its laser-ray strength blasting the gray clay of an endless dead-level horizon. These were the conditions that found a small ceremonial group of us standing in the midst of this massive, vacuous prehistoric lakebed surrounding a slight but oh-so tall gold spike that marked the exact center of Black Rock City. The playa was a pristine canvas, and all of our imaginations struggled to superimpose this forthcoming color-city of fire onto it. Impossible, it seemed — but we'd been there before, faced with the same titanic task. I remember standing with sort of a half-mast gaze, thinking this would be the monumental achievement of my lifetime.

When the core group of our well-wishing comrades left us in their rugged vehicles riding on ever shrinking dust plumes like witches' brooms, we were left with nothing but ourselves, a well-supplied school bus, the total and inescapable burning drill of the sun, and the unyielding, maddening, solid blast of the south wind. It really doesn't get any better! One by one, the flags started going in and the giant curve of Black Rock City became the face of the eclipsed sun, slowly emerging from behind a black moon. Hello, old friend. So we meet again. 🔥

Tony Perez

don't know how to dream

without you lying near

do you recall the face of burning tears?

hand in hand in that last improbable dance

soon after you were gone / crying tears of sand

one year later the faces couldn't be found

in their place was yours ...

out of the dust emerging

tears carving through dust to skin

in this place / last year became yesterday

skin not grass covering you

brass not flame

driftwood not sand

this playa / our land

Andrew Moore

from **Burning Man Hell**

Thursday, August 29
    10:30 am

            caravan
        two vans loaded

lawn chair, umbrella, inflatable mattress, sleeping bag, pillow
70 gallons water, paper towels, baby wipes, toilet tissues
bowls, plates, knife, fork, spoon, wine, mushrooms, sweet rolls
peanut butter, jelly, coffee, eight cans of tuna, lettuce, tomato, bread
Diet Pepsi, peanuts, pretzels, biscotti, sun block, ear plugs, flashlight
candles, hat, Chapstick, garbage bags, can opener, 4 bicycles

        Tiki torches

Michael Rothenberg

Santas? Or Clowns?

Out in the middle of the desert, far away from anything else, there is a strange little line in the playa. Late at night it can look imaginary. Some fanciful illusion, or perhaps a piece of art expressing random amusement.

Eight little structures, each like a crossbreed between a tollbooth and a very large standing lamp, make up four little gates. No fence extends on either side. This imaginary line in the desert is all that separates you from the people coming to play with you.

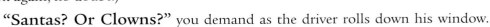

In some sense it's amazing they come to you at all, given the width of the playa and the depth of the night. But all the tracks seem to be going towards you and you are the closest light source. (The basic moth-like instinct of humankind at work again, no doubt.)

"Santas? Or Clowns?" you demand as the driver rolls down his window.

The head shakes a little as it turns towards you with a mix of weariness and distraction. **"Huh?"** he asks.

"Santas or Clowns?" you reply as if it's perfectly obvious at this point, as it should be to anyone paying halfway decent attention.

"It's really the most important question, and we just have to know. Are you with the Santas?" You wave towards a group of St. Nicks nearby in full antic prowl. **"Or are you with the Clowns?"** You point towards the rear at something which has clearly begun distracting him again.

You really must get his attention again soon. You have many important pieces of information to somehow wedge into his subconscious so that he will be a wonderful, happy, willing and responsible participant in the community he is about to join.

There are important questions to ask, too! Like, does he know where he's going to be camping? He's a very tired puppy because he was packing all last night and trying to get everything ready to leave today and then he drove all night. And, well, behind you in the city are a lot of very distracted people without particularly good light sources, and you want to make sure that he doesn't begin any random acquaintances with his chrome bumpers.

Of course, the most important question is, **"Have you ever been to Burning Man?"** It's best asked in a sincere voice so as to get a truthful answer because it will let you know how much you get to fuck with him.

When he tells you he's never been to Burning Man before, you sing out, **"He's a VIRGIN!"** before he's had a chance to contemplate his error. Oh look! He's distracted again.

"Excuse me," you ask. **"Have you heard your lesson about the Port-a-potties yet?"**

The head swings back towards you, back to the distraction, and back to you again. **"Huh?"**

"The Port-a-potties! It's very important." As you hand him a packet of useful information and inflict upon him messages about dust control, Rangers, water, stuff you've seen and a general sense of where he is currently located relative to other stuff, flocks of mad Santas are swirling by outside, scrambling over his hood, and hitting on his girlfriend.

He's not paying very good attention to you. Especially since the most disturbing clown he's ever seen in his life has begun striding forcefully towards his vehicle.

"Are these Santas distracting you? If you're having trouble internalizing any of these important details here, I can always send in the clowns," you say, shaking your head like a woeful schoolmarm.

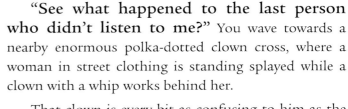

"See what happened to the last person who didn't listen to me?" You wave towards a nearby enormous polka-dotted clown cross, where a woman in street clothing is standing splayed while a clown with a whip works behind her.

That clown is every bit as confusing to him as the enormous one in the black leather loincloth and black boots who is now shoving his bold red nose in the window and smiling. "A virgin, eh? What took you so long to get here?"

As his girlfriend disappears into the night with a Santa in drag he starts laughing. The stress of getting here is over. The long drive is over. And it's all okay. These escapees from a lunatic asylum who apparently wield some sort of precarious authority, are telling him "important things" and inspecting his water supply.

He looks up. "Santa," he finally answers. "Definitely, I'm with the Santas."

You see his shoulders relax as the laughter shakes through him.

"I'm here, aren't I?" he asks almost in wonder. "I'm at Burning Man!" he whoops.

"Welcome home," you grin, indicating the magical city ahead.

As the next car stirs idle dust towards you, you race to the window and shriek, "Santas? Or Clowns!?" 🔥

Katrina Glerum

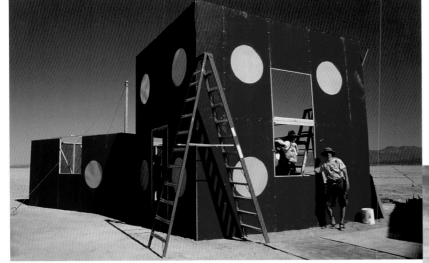

bman-byou

Burning Man
Burning Land
Burning Hands
Burning Fans

Build Art
Build Dreams
Build Mystery
Build Schemes

Bright Nights
Bright Minds
Bright Stars
Bright Blinds.

Beauty Lives.
Beauty Dies.
Beauty Mutates.
Beauty Cries.

Be Bold
Be Gay
Be tomorrow ...
Be today.

Burn past;
Burn Possession.
Burn ferocious;
Burn Regression.

Be Alive.
Be true
Be shameless
Be you.

Burning Futures
Burning Plans
Burning Hearts
Burning Man

Vicki Olds (shibumi)

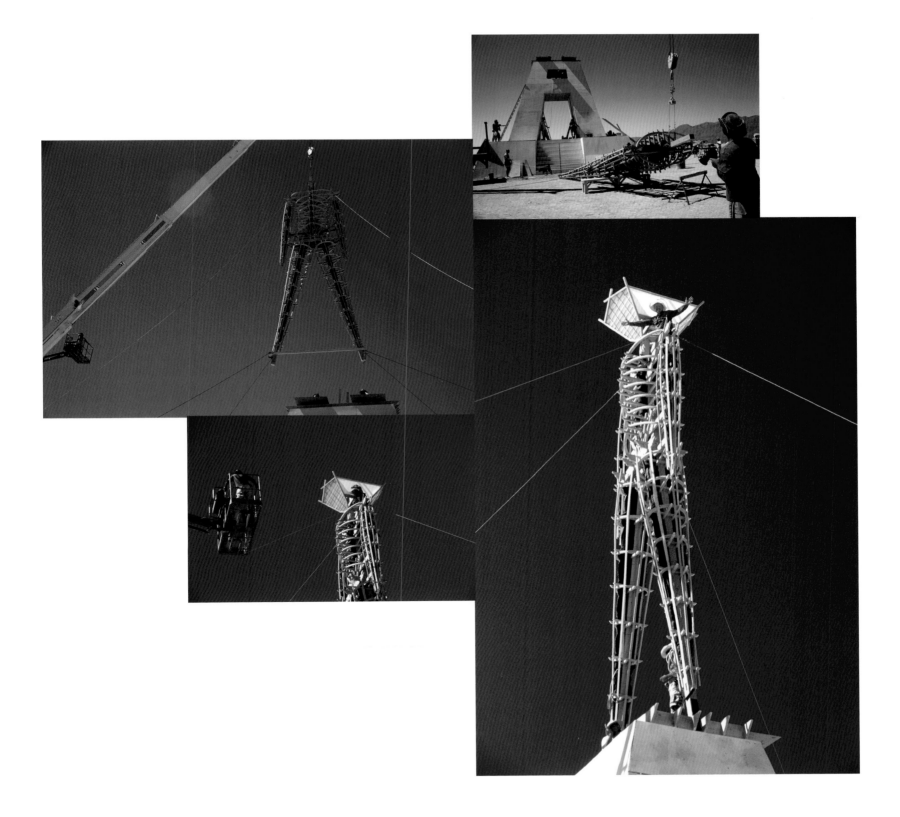

Reflection '94

We wander towards the center of town, first stopping by the beautiful sculpture of the Man, and then down the promenade, as night begins. We hear the sound of drums, first just a few, then several more, beating out tribal rhythms. A procession starts and people begin to gather and walk with the wandering drummers. Fire breathers join us and we all follow the gathering crowd to the iconic Burning Man totem. There is dancing and drumming, clothing becomes optional, and at the base of the Man three women dance in traditional butoh form with a slow, impassioned intensity. At the other end of the circle, bare-breasted dancers writhe passionately in a trance-dance invocation of sex and fire. The drumming has increased and small gongs join with clapping hands all around. The two dances move to the center but never meet. The stage is set; its tension is very real.

The dancers lead us to a 30 foot-high chimney built of chicken wire and clay whose vulval opening is crowned by a pointed phallus. The chimney, packed with dry wood, is lit. As the clay heats it becomes transparent. The 30-foot phallus glows red and writhes with dancing flames crawling up its exterior. At the top, fireworks explode, sending showers of sparks into the shuddering crowd. We are red-hot. We are yelling. We are willing the dissolution and fall of this beautiful and powerful object. It kneels with a graceful swoop, exploding the circle, which reforms into a dance spiraling around the bonfire. This moment is exultant as we dance in the blinding heat.

The rest of the evening has lighter diversions: a masked play; a mesmerizing dragon sculpture spitting 15-foot flames; a slow ballet of exploding fireworks strapped to three well-insulated performers. And to finish, the presentation of dummy clowns stuffed with all sorts of pyrotechnic devices. These are the simulacrum of the Burning Man drawn with humor and no less danger. Explosions scatter the crowd while a punk band wails, "Everybody likes a clown, especially a flaming clown!"

I'm thinking about the Burning Man — what it is and who we are in relationship to it. There are many archetypal signposts here — the invocation of Kali, the burning bush, the death of summer (and of the king), the funeral pyre, the purification of the flame, the point of clarity reached by blinding heat, the exorcism of so many things and the phoenix rising from the ashes. And we're the desert dwellers, the wandering Jews, the spontaneous anarchist utopia, a singular tribe of brothers and sisters wired by shared experience and libation. This is innocence regained through experience.

The next day, the Man is lowered to the ground for pyrotechnic preparation. Guy lines and ropes are checked, as is the gasoline-soaked burlap that fill the arms and legs of the Man and the plethora of explosive fireworks hidden everywhere in the finely made wooden structure. A firefighter installs a smoke detector at the sculpture's genitalia — a wry joke, to be sure — and nails a folded American flag just below

the sternum in memory of firefighters who died in the past year. We latch upon the thick rope that will pull him erect in the now dark twilight. Millions of stars shatter the sky like crushed diamonds strewn upon velveteen. Here, like some anarchist barn-raising, with a great whoop and holler, the erection of this beautiful icon grows out of our collective labor. The blue neon skeleton is lit, the drums speed their course and the crowd cheers with joy.

There are uncertain moments when the neon flickers on, off and on again. The spectacle at his feet is less tenuous. A man and a woman, bodies adorned with swirling tattoos, make wide arcs around the Man wielding torches and eventually lighting him. What else is there to describe? The sparks, the explosions, the fire, the heat, the drums, the fall and crash, the implosion of the dance, the explosion of the energy, the revelation of the spirit, the rhythm continuing, reassembling. Both Dionysus and Pan join the revelry. 🔥

Mark Jan Wlodarkiewicz

Warmth

The stars are glad
that my eyes can see them

so too the wind,
that feels along my face

I am made more at home
in the desert

than ever I was
in your arms

R.A. Robertson

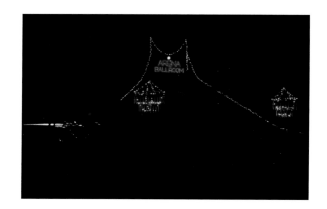

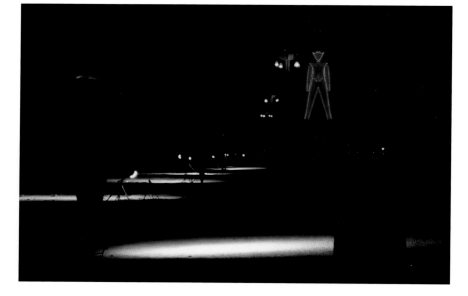

All that is solid

In this crucible of alkali
Ringed by mountains that once formed
the shores of an ancient sea
There are dinosaurs evaporating into the atmosphere
A final brilliant release
After millennia of internment.
And the flora of the pre-conscious world
Are boiling into space

I wonder if some molecule
in all that propane
was once part of a fern palm
Casting a shadow
on another once part of a coelacanth
Gliding beneath the shimmering surface
of the cool black rock sea.

Ian McFarland

Nameless

Celebrating a god who shall remain nameless

Creating a faith that can remain blameless

Acknowledging all that we know is divine

Is the artistry in your life the light and love in mine

Reminding myself of the reasons for living

Laughing loving learning giving

Building a city in the soul of a nation

That's what I did on my summer vacation

Reed Hortie

from **Big Al's Lonertown Tours**

The Quiet Side Tour

Take this solitary tour to the southern end of Black Rock City;
don't stop at Neptune, but keep on going to the outer limits
of the Southland. Feel the desolation as you move into a realm
reserved for the occasional naked pissing guy, and a variety of
quietly vigilant artwork. Gaze at the creativity that also desires
to be alone, and feel at home in the absence of others.

Allison Yates

night falls on the Playa

and I wander and wonder

don't know where I'm going

but let me just travel

here

      there

            everywhere

                  nowhere

sand in my shoes, in every part of Me

I pass the hourglass, captive time

momentous memories alive in sculpture

                    alive in Me

music in the air. the beat draws me to It

signpost through the Desert, cacophonous compass

I arrive in The Flow:

        I Burn, I Heal

I AM

    a stream

      IN the Conscious Nation

              AND SO I DANCE

in the House of the Universe ...

and to my surprise

day dawns on the Playa.

Anne L. Francis

I Understand

I've seen truth

I've seen heaven

I've seen myself

Standing on the sun

I've seen light

I've seen sound

I've seen myself

Standing in the dream

I've seen reality

I've seen fantasy

I've seen myself

As I truly am

I've seen beauty

I've seen purity

I've seen the world

As it truly should be

Sean McKnight

I Dream of a Tie-Dyed Wind Sock

What would you think it might be like to bike headlong into a menacing, swirling dust devil? In the past, I would have hardly thought my greatest concern would be avoiding the five other bicyclists chasing the same thrill. But then again, normal expectations just aren't very useful at Burning Man.

After all, when was the last time you saw a neon momma kangaroo hopping along in the darkness, her baby bouncing just a step behind? My mind tells me that there must be people involved somehow, but I can't see them. I can only see the exquisite blue and red and yellow and green outlines of the marsupials as they disappear into the ethereal warm playa night.

I feel tears welling up sometimes as I think about the creativity and generosity of the thousands of artists who spend probably more time and money than they can realistically afford getting ready for Burning Man, just so their friends and neighbors will smile and laugh and cry.

During a week in Black Rock City, everyone seems to weather the full range of their emotions; it's not just the harsh desert heat or unexpected cold, and it's not just the lack of sleep or food. I think it's got more to do with the fact that modern people really weren't meant to be dropped into the middle of a desert for a week, no matter how much water or beef jerky they cart with them. So when I see two good friends overwhelmed from fatigue and lack of nourishment and thirst screaming at each other, I know it's just a prelude to their lovely moment of reconciliation, when the two will realize the absurdity of their anger and they'll embrace and laugh and shake it off and cook and eat together and take long pulls on their water bottles and then run off to play like children.

I can see them, off in the distance. It's getting dark, but they've climbed up on a playground slide bathed in black light, and they're shooting down like an avalanche and tumbling to a stop, and rushing to do it again. But before they can climb back up they're distracted by the sounds of an art car rolling by with a gaggle of folks dressed like butterflies hanging from a metal frame erected over a three-level couch and yelling at them to climb on board. The slide forgotten, they mount the bus-of-sorts and I won't see them again until I discover them the next morning, passed out, their legs not quite folded into their tent.

As for me, I'm discovering the joys of the playa at night. I climb aboard my trusty beater bike and point it north and close my eyes and spread my wings and pedal and listen to the sounds of the wheels as they shoot across the jet-black playa. I know it's dangerous: I could easily collide with something — possibly someone else pitching blindly into the night on a bike. But what are the odds? The playa is vast and empty and I've got good ears and I don't hear anything near me. All I hear is the fusion of sounds of fun back in Black Rock City behind me and so I ride and ride until finally, I realize my equilibrium is off and I'm going to fall over and I jam on the brakes and my eyes open and I'm face to face with something I can hardly explain: a long, gorgeous, tie-dyed wind sock, snapping in the wind, big enough for me, and beckoning me in.

I remember this. I saw it during the day, a line of people waiting to walk through it, kids and parents and grandparents squealing happily as they scrambled through that life-size T-shirt wrapped into a giant cylinder. It is the smoothest fabric I can imagine, and it is a pleasure just to run my fingers along it. In daylight, the colors of the tie-dye sparkle with life and love and imagination as the sun bursts through from above. At night it's more subdued, with the city lights behind me barely illuminating the brilliance of the artist's creation. But now no one else is around, and so I enter and I lie down and I reach out and ensconce myself in the cool fabric and it's like a happy, fulfilling, all-encompassing dream. My mind fills in the colors and my eyes are bombarded with a cacophony of bright hues.

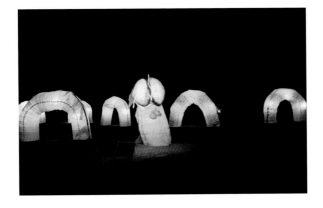

I feel like I could lay here all night without anyone finding me, but a group of 50 people clad all in red arrives on a rolling bar car, boisterous with booze, loud with tales and eager to dash through my home of the moment. They rush in and say hello and nimbly avoid me as they crash a little drunkenly towards the far end of the wind sock and I don't mind that they're there, of course, because now I can hoist my beater on their bar car, pop open the cold beer I know they're going to hand me and cruise in style back towards the city.

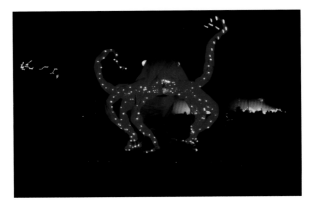

I'll surely make new friends here: men and women and boys and girls from San Francisco and Anchorage and Padua, Italy, with names I've never heard and haircuts I've never seen and I'll wonder why they're all dressed in red but I'll forget to ask and they'll invite me along with them to the fire performance they heard about. They're not sure where it is or even when it is, for that matter — someone says it could have been last night or it might be tomorrow — but no matter. If we roll along far enough, we're sure to find some fire. This is Burning Man!

I look around at the group and I've never seen so many smiles in one place, and one of them is mine. But I decide it's time for me to move on again, so as we slow to lure some pedestrians with the siren call of a cold cerveza, cerveza, cerveza! I hop off, get back on the beater and point myself like an arrow for the Center Café, which on this crisp, clear night — it must be four or five in the morning by now, I decide — is lit with so many lights and colors and is so bursting with life that you might imagine they're in there preparing a space shuttle for launch.

I'm a little tired and thirsty, so I stand in a short line and talk to some young lady with a ravishing Kiwi accent about this art or that costume and finally I get my hot chocolate and I'm happy. I sit for a bit and see some friends and we talk, but I'm distracted: there's so much out there I need to see and though it'll be there tomorrow and the day after that, I'm antsy, so I excuse myself and hop back on the beater and I ride toward the sound of a rave off in the distance.

When I get there, I find 20 or 30 Burners gyrating to a sound system, and I dismount and I throw the bike down and I charge right in. I close my eyes and I dance and I dance and I move to the beat and it envelopes me. My mind fills as the sounds evolve into images, images of the things I've seen today and yesterday and the things I know I'll see tomorrow and I think, there's no place like this. When you arrive at Burning Man you're greeted with signs that say Welcome Home, and it's true, and I'm mimicking the Wizard of Oz, mumbling **There's No Place Like Home, There's No Place Like Home,** and a few people hear me and they laugh and give me the thumbs up, and we dance together and I'm sweating and feeling good and the music is infectious and I want it to last forever when I notice that I've danced myself out onto the open playa and I'm by myself again and I must walk.

So I leave my beater there, and I see some fireballs roaring into the blackened sky and I race out to see what's going on. Before I know it, I'm in the middle of a crowd of hundreds watching a man (or is it a woman?) in a silver fire suit shooting huge plumes of flame a million feet into the sky and with each blast, the crowd lets out a gigantic, orgasmic cheer that surrounds me like the wind sock and makes me want to shout

and cry and scream and fall down and laugh and I notice that people around me are doing all those things and the next blast turns the darkness into an inferno and everything is orange and red and yellow and the cheer rises again.

And I look at the horizon and I see the tops of the mountains starting to betray the first signs of what will surely be the most beautiful sunrise I've ever seen — at least since yesterday — and out on the edge of the Esplanade I watch a troupe of fire-spinners writhing and gyrating impossibly and together, the early risers and the up-all-nighters are dancing and celebrating the start of the new day and I'm reminded of how the day before, after 48 hours of muddy rain and debilitating wind, the sun broke through the clouds above Black Rock City and all at once, 26,000 people climbed out of their motor homes and tents and vans and domes and saw the beautiful sunlight streaking down towards us and without knowing what we were doing, the entire city let out a full-bodied joyous roar. In every direction, all I could see was

people with their arms raised above their heads, jumping up and down and up and down and relief that the storm was over washed through the city and we were alive! 🔥

Daniel Terdiman

You can't, you can't see everything. You can't do everything. To pursue coherence. Oh yeah, wow. Looks just like the Persian Gulf War. Evening. Allo...een. Running around. Replication occurs. It blows my mind. Two 300-foot canvases out there. Kinetic. They'll just lift right off the ground. Tra-la-la. Ahhhhh it's the Barbie Car. So, you look lovely in a blonde wig. It is my natural color, other than green. I haven't been out there yet. I know. I wish. Reflected...the...individual. Oh, so it's not lit. Closure and beginning. Esplanade? Whoa, you can see, you can see, you can see. Oh yay, the Tesla coil. Dragons above...head. I'm so glad, yes it is. Stop that feather! Woops, sorry. It's quite all right. Stand back. Affords protection. Stand back. It's gonna light. You wanna...3...darkness. What happens when you look up? Very nice. Thank you for sharing.

Identities—memories—they may be told and retold
The new always appears in the cloak of awareness
The unhampered pursuit and the process itself
Deeds and words find to a degree what they were lacking
in the thoughts and accounts of others
Completion through the sheer force of trained, but
released, imagination

To feel as if these words, "Good Morning," were
inserted in the middle of a conversation
It is difficult to begin at the beginning
What—is steadfast, constant
Containing some evidence, but of a very scattered kind
To see through the two eyes—shall also see them
if looking upon

In a minute, you can hear the dust settle
Weight that overpowers, touched by such
The new-found sentience—it's getting dark, so light
Tears blur eyes—the clarity of hearing

Travis Ortiz

Wandering around at night following

our whimsy
a bright light
a welcoming sound

We come across Orbit
surrounded by a crowd
half of which is lying on its back looking up
while the standers spin the three mounted spheres around
in different directions
to the sound
        of giggling
            giggling
                giggling from those lying down

After the spheres stop themselves a man sits and yells:
"Look everybody, look what someone did for us! Thank you somebody for doing this"

Rita Manachi

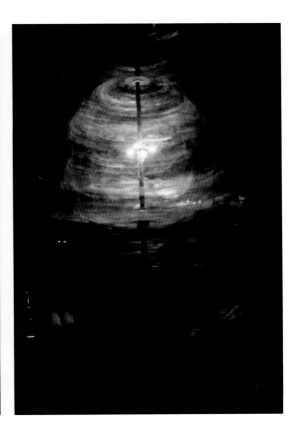

from **Terza Preghiera**

a kinetic poetry (spoon) sculpture

¹☉ 8° ♍

²I feel your splendor.
³I think we want connection.
⁴I have the courage to share.

⁵♂ 10° ♏

⁶I perceive you as part of me.
⁷I know we are travelers.
⁸I know we've met before.

⁹♆ 27° ♑ ʀ

¹⁰I create an atmosphere of love.
¹¹I will peace.
¹²I feel the mystery of nature.
¹³I analyze the unknown.

¹⁴♀ 16° ♎

¹⁵I am part of us all.
¹⁶I perceive many as one.

¹⁷♄ 19° ♈ ʀ

¹⁸I know everything will be fine.
¹⁹I believe in beauty.
²⁰I create a life of magic.
²¹I will the absence of hunger.

²²☽ 21° ♌

²³I analyze the forbidden.
²⁴I have tolerance for resistance.
²⁵I create a safe place, safe space.

²⁶♃ 14° ♒

²⁷I use delicacy.
²⁸I know it's a shared dream.
²⁹I believe we'll meet again.
³⁰I create passion.
³¹I will the strong to care for the weak.
³²I feel an innocence among us.

³³☿ 8° ♍ ʀ

³⁴I balance intellect with emotion.
³⁵I am blessed to be.
³⁶I perceive your knowing.
³⁷I use my power for good.

³⁸♅ 5° ♒ ʀ

³⁹I believe in manifestation.
⁴⁰I create my everything.

M. Mara-Ann

Let me be dangerous

Let me stand in the back of a pickup truck as it does sixty mph down
the highway, flamethrowers blazing as propane tanks roll around my feet
Let me work on the top rung of the ladder, in a duststorm, at night
Let twenty thousand volts course around me
Let me fall in love with a stranger I'll never see again
Let me unshackle the leash that keeps me safe, that protects me from myself, that makes youth long for war
Let me be bound with the links of shared hardship
Let me risk for art's sake, for the city, for foolish fun
Let me dance with knives
Let me play with fire

I jumped up to the back of the forklift, balanced above wheels as tall as I am.
"Mind if I catch a ride?" I asked.
"You fall, you die," the driver answered.
"That's fair," I said.

John Kelly

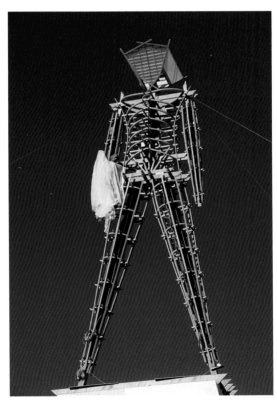

disowning

1.

go to the desert
lie down on
what the map
would show to
be a line

pick yourself up
find another line
lie down
get up

erase all the
lines this way
and that

think of it as
a poem without
line without
lines between
lines

think of it as
picking up
a lie

pos	word	freq
1	disowning	1
2	go	2
3	to	6
4	the	21
5	desert	2
6	lie	3
7	down	4
8	on	4
9	what	2
10	map	1
11	would	1
12	show	1
13	be	1
14	a	6
15	line	3
16	pick	2
17	yourself	2
18	up	6
19	find	1
20	another	1
21	get	1
22	erase	1
23	all	2
24	lines	3
25	this	1
26	way	
27	and	
28	that	
29	think	
30	of	
31	it	
32	as	
33	poem	
34	without	
35	between	
36	picking	
37	train	
38	your	
39	eyes	
40	horizon	
41	page	
42	walk	
43	away	
44	from	
45	every	
46	thing	
47	else	
48	look	
49	where	
50	words	2
51	fall	1
52	beneath	1
53	you	4
54	run	1
55	finger	2
56	eye	1
57	follows	2
58	stop	1
59	around	1
60	now	1
61	then	1
86	blank	2
87	at	1
88	end	1
89	book	2
90	closing	2
91	steps	1

	pos	freq
93	mountains	1
94	sand	1
95	off	1
96	land	1
97	out	1

eye	1	56
eyes	3	39
fall	1	51
find	1	19
finger	2	55
floor	1	73

2.

train your eyes
on the horizon
of the page

walk away from
it and every
thing else

train your eyes
to look down to
where words
fall away
beneath you

run your finger
down the page
and away from
the horizon

your eye follows
the finger the
horizon follows
your eyes

sand	1	94
shadow	1	75
show	1	12
shrubs	1	71
small	1	68
steps	1	91
stop	1	58
take	1	62
that	1	28
the	21	4
then	1	61
thin	1	70
thing	1	46
think	3	29
this	1	25
to	6	3
train	2	37
up	6	18
valleys	1	67
walk	2	42

disowning	1	1
down	4	7
else	1	47
end	1	88
erase	1	22
every	1	45

pick	2	16
picking	2	36
poem	1	33
punctuation	1	8
run	1	54
said	1	64

	pos	freq
way	1	26
what	2	9
where	1	49
who	1	77
wind	1	85
without	2	34
words	2	50
would	1	11
you	4	53

your	5	38
yourself	2	17

21x (1)
the

10x (1)
and

7x (1)
of

3.   6x (4)
stop a to up your to look
around   now
and 4x (5) then to
take as down on page back what
you you said

the 3x (8) names
on   all   the
away eyes horizon it lie line lines think
peaks   and
valleys 2x (18)
all blank book closing desert finger follows from
the go look pick picking train walk what small
burrows
without words yourself
and   thin
shrubs
burning
on 1x (59) the desert
after another around
floor
at back backwards be before beneath
between blowing
pick   up   after
burning
yourself and
burrows by departed disowning else end erase every eye
the   shadow of
fall find floor get in land
others   who
loose map mountains now names off
departed
others out peaks poem
before   you
punctuation run said
the sand loose
shadow show shrubs
punctuation
small steps stop take
blowing   by
that then thin thing
in   the   wind
this valleys way where
who wind world
the the the the the the

on on on on

page page page page you

you you you

4.

the the the the the the the the the
the the the the the the

away away away
a   blank   page

eyes eyes eyes
think   of   a   blank
page   at   the
horizon horizon horizon
end   of   a   book

and and and and and and and and and and

it it it lie lie lie
closing   the   book
and   picking   up
line line line lines lines lines
your   steps   as

of of of of of of of

think think think
backwards
you   go
all all blank blank book book

a a a a a a

closing   up
closing closing desert desert
the   mountains
and   sand   as
finger finger follows follows
you   walk   off
the   land   and   out
from from go go look look
of   the   words.
pick

to to to to to to up up up up up up

William Fox
pick pick picking picking

your your your your your your

train train walk walk what

as as as as

what without without words words

down down down down

yourself yourself

after another around at back backwards be
before beneath between blowing burning
burrows by departed disowning else end

erase every eye fall find floor get in land
loose map mountains now names off others
out peaks poem punctuation run said sand
shadow show shrubs small steps stop take
that then thin thing this valleys way where
who wind world

"How was it?" she asks, and attempts are made.

Everywhere tiny lights, that's how it was.

Spindly beds and silken tents, tasseled, strung up pink in the night.

"Imagine the gentlest thing," I say, and it was gentler.

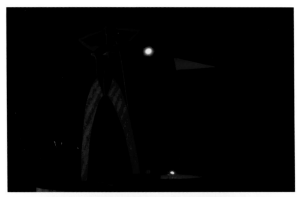

"What's it like?" she wants to know.

Like hot iron hearts, giant metal bellows. The engine room of a war ship on Mars.

Broomstick plumes, black umbra shot far into a broad irregular band of stars.

It's like only itself, which wants most to be unlike itself — large;

and if you really would know,

Walk into a dust storm — look for a starched lace shrine.

Be as a purposeful ghost, with no use for metaphor and

Appetite for both fire and brine, having died last night — wanting badly to watch

Death itself burn, drown. Go down.

Find the eidolons in ball gowns, waltzing through one another in pairs

At the bottom of a dry lakebed in hours when animals speak —

Insane with their grief and passing into delight,

    these wraiths put off red and blue sequin sparks in the night.

They are deeply, sincerely and profoundly polite.

That is what it's like.

That is what it's like.

Shannon Coulter

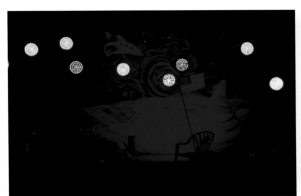

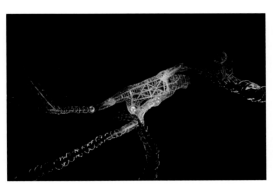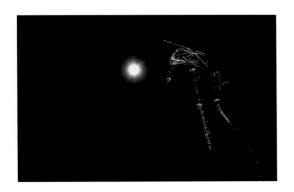

I tumble out of my tent like a pile of
unwashed socks into the laundryroom night, where
all is dark, whirling and buzzing. In the distance a
thousand parties giggle and rumble. Reds, greens and blues pulsate in
patterns on the horizon, like a bank of mission-control buttons I can't wait to press.

My tent partner is nowhere to be seen. No matter; she can't have gone further than a mile or two. First things first — grope the foggy earth for dust-crusted sandals, stretch daysleep-curled muscles into the infinite sky. Feel the benefit. Taste the possibilities. Find the flashlight.

Once I assemble torch and waterpack, the two-way radio dangling from my velcro waist-towel starts making noises. When it feels like it, this device is my Plastic Man arm, reaching out into the city, yanking up friends and creating random collisions of humanity. But tonight it just hisses and beeps like a fearsome electronic snake. Clearly, the Universe sees a quest in my immediate future.

It reinforces this point seconds later when my neighbors show up in a chauffeur-driven golf cart with purple fur trim and a naked torso photo collage on the hood. The cart's owner, his delivery completed, is questless and eager; a Sancho Panza seeking his next Don Quixote. I explain my windmill-tilting desire: to venture deep, deep into the playa until we reach two 16-foot-high red dice. Though Sancho has never seen the dice, there is no need to argue over their existence or explain their even more improbable contents — a prohibition-era casino and jazz club (where, if all goes well, my tent partner will be found). Sancho accepts and understands implicitly. In fact, he's so jazzed he wants me to drive. All of a sudden this total stranger and his mutant purple torso chariot are mine to command. I drive gleefully, like I've never driven before — indeed, I have never driven a mutant vehicle before — in seasick waves and the occasional loop-the-loop, savoring the drive more than reaching the destination.

Outside the Dice is a parking lot of exotic, anthropomorphic people-carriers: dragons and butterflies and winged dinosaurs, oh my. Inside is the usual crowd of thirsty crazies, all of whom have latched on to the premise — for the gift of a drink, they must offer a gift of their own. We make them do magic tricks or spin fire naked; whatever talent they have to offer, we tease it out. Right now one of the good doctors from Spock Mountain Research is dispensing his patented Hyperwhisky while a guy in moth wings and fez is regaling the crowd with tales of his childhood. My favorite customers are the ones who have the chutzpah to walk into the Dice for the first time, size up the situation, and without batting an eyelid ask the barkeep for "my usual." **That's what Burning Man is all about: instant participatory fantasy.**

My tent partner, I am told, is looking for me just as eagerly as I am looking for her; in fact, she just went back to the tent. So I hitch another ride, this time from a guy with red horns and a pitchfork. The only space for me is on the back of his steed, so I'm hanging off the back of a chariot driven at demonic speed by the devil himself. We're both whooping with joy as the lights and lasers of Black Rock approach, and I'm thinking: if only Jerry Falwell could see us now.

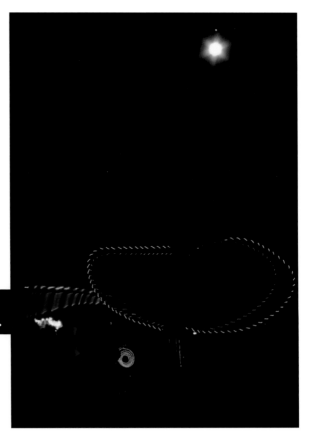

The tent is empty. My neighbors tell me my tent partner has gone back to the Dice again. **There's a lot of this kind of thing going on at Burning Man, but it never really seems to be a big deal.** Nobody ever gets upset at the need to make a journey; nobody cares about making appointments on time. How could you, with this kind of synchronistic, never-a-dull-ride taxi service?

So I'm heading back to the Dice on the back of a giant bomb, feeling like Slim Pickens in Dr. Strangelove. There's a faint glimmer of gold on the empty horizon. What time is it? Doesn't matter. Playa time. And finally, there she is — tending bar at the dog-end of the night, chatting to the regulars, eyes as twinkle-filled as ever. The live jazz band has wound down, the chanteuse pours a hefty draft of pain into one last ballad, and if the Dice club fantasy were truly complete, someone would be sweeping sadly in the corner, stacking chairs and dreaming of a better life. Only there is nothing to sweep up (leave no trace) and no better life to dream of.

We drive back to camp with the Dice club staff as the sun starts piercing the sky with its own unimpeachable laser. Before we head away from the **dawn and back to the sleeping city, our driver makes several wild loops of the giant red bones. Just to be sure.** 🔥

Chris Taylor

from **17 Lines for 7 Ages:** A Ballad to Burning Man 2001

Everything is composed of many parts.

Everything is part of something else.

Fertilized with memories I bring on a blooming springtime of the mind.

Clear Menser

Go now.

Go now. Whatever it is
that you long for is waiting for you
Right now.
How can you be so bad
to make it keep waiting?

In this moment I dropped
another small burden
saw a little more
of myself.
Whatever it is:
you can simply drop it
and go on freely.

Whoever it is you think you have to be
is not as dear as you
right now. Know nothing.
We are here.

Ron Meiners

Together

That we appear

    separate

is the illusion.

At one time

    the desert was

a mountain.

And we were children.

Tom Kramer

The desert has

a way of twisting

Dreams into reality

Darkness into light

Swaying us to joy

And love

Let's not forget the lessons

Learned in the vastness

As the Angry Giant shifts and turns into life

Sleeping burden of light and liberty

As all mundane seems inconsequential

Our lives fill with hope

For a brighter day

Jay Kravitz

Black Rock Desert Desserts

Part I: Minimum Requirements

Astrologer Richard Geer, a wise maniac I met in Toronto, once asked me, "What are your minimum requirements for living in paradise right here on Earth?" At the time I wasn't sure. Now that I've been at Burning Man, I know. Here they are:

A lush profusion of exuberant art spawned in the spirit of love and generosity, unmediated by the distortions of commerce;

Regular arrivals of new allies, who come together with me to foment a sexy overthrow of whatever status quo most needs to be overthrown;

A growing tribe of like-minded creators committed to changing or at least adding onto our names regularly, so that our identities are always in frothy flux.

We who live in paradise continually make up and remake our own idiosyncratic spiritual path by borrowing from all the spiritual paths; we throw our weight behind the righteous cause of nurturing six billion different religions on planet Earth; we burn down the shrines at which we worshiped last month or last year so that we become sufficiently empty and humble to receive the fresh raw blessings coming from divine sources we have never before been able to conceive of, let alone register.

Part II: Narrative

It's the early evening of Saturday, a few hours before the 60-foot wooden and neon effigy known as the Man will be consumed in flames. I'm at the Plastic Chapel, not too far from the Man, where priests and priestesses

of every variety have presided over weddings all week. A few of the ceremonies have been legal in the eyes of the state. But most are temporary, or are little more than ironic fucking licenses, or have joined together conclaves of polyamorous experimentalists for whom a two-person union is not inclusive enough.

Rising up starkly from the flat gray-brown desert, teased by short-lived miniature dust tornadoes, the two-story-high Plastic Chapel is made of brightly colored pieces of plastic salvaged from dumps and junkyards all over Nevada. It's a vision of wacky loveliness. On the south wall, for instance, there's a green toy shovel and red jelly sandal and shards of a pink Barbie car melted together and jutting out of the orange and purple facade like a bas-relief.

As a crowd gathers below, I'm puttering around a stage carved out of the second-story of the Plastic Chapel. With three fellow musicians, I'm preparing to perform a pagan revival show that will culminate in an ecstatic wedding ceremony. The rite will be unique. In a benevolent inversion of the bizarre mass marriages

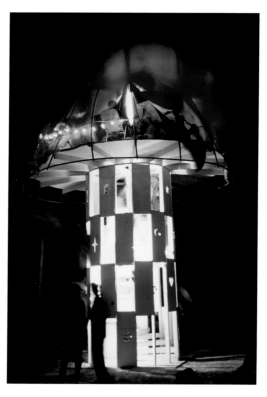

conducted by cult leader Sun Myung Moon, we will sanctify the conjugal union of every audience member to himself or herself: a mass self-wedding.

I have never in my life felt surrounded by such relaxing fertility, by so much luxuriant conviviality. For many days now I have glided without even a taint of fear through a city of 25,000 people. Unknown allies and I have spotted each other from a block away and run to each other like long-lost friends from previous incarnations. Besieged by magnanimous strangers bearing no-strings-attached blessings — free massages, free absinthe, free rides in a Viking ship on wheels, free spreads of gourmet Greek cuisine, free kisses — I find myself yearning to give away everything I own. I have been in love with more than a few women in my life, but this is the first time I've plunged into the throes of spiritual infatuation with a time and place.

"You are a fucking genius," we sing to everyone in the crowd below us at the Plastic Chapel. "The fullness of your divine charisma is erupting from your uncanny heart. You know the difference between stupid suffering and wise suffering. You are so in tune with your own destiny that you can be yourself even when you are beside yourself." Coated with dust and decorated with paint and glitter, our co-worshipers' faces are open and clear. Tears stream down some cheeks like rain coursing through dry riverbeds. Many of their bodies are naked or barely clad. Others wear gold top hats or silk pantaloons or ancient Egyptian breastplates or velvet frock coats. In the distance, a festive caravan of equally blithe spirits flows steadily towards the as-yet-unburned Man, who is enjoying his final hours as an enigmatic icon about two hundred yards from us.

We of the Sacred Uproar spin our prayers, songs, sermons, prophecies, and invocations for more than an hour. The full moon's light now shines brighter than the waning sun. We can see the dancers who will ignite the fire beginning to circle around the Man. Soon he'll be in flames. It's time for our denouement here at the Plastic Chapel.

As the Lush Confuser and the Holy Healing Bitch weave hair-raising harmonies that exactly match the color of the spectral light, as the Maniacal Miracle-Maker unleashes a gushing music of the spheres I swear I heard in my dream last night, I lead the devotees through the climax:

"And now I ask you to hold your own hand," I chant. "Close your eyes and imagine gazing into a mirror. And repeat the following sacred vows to yourself. 'I will never forsake you. I will never betray you. I will forgive you for your imperfections and praise you for your beauty. I will always treat you with reverence and respect.

"'I will love you until the end of time. I will do with you what the spring does to the cherry trees.'

"I now pronounce you your own husband and your own wife, married to yourself in the eyes of the Goddess, forever and ever. You may kiss yourself on your own lips." ◌

Rob Brezsny

my heart has been burned clean

I have fallen both in and out of love
behind my often dreaming eyes

the desert
cracked earth
is the landscape of my imagination
it is as real as the transparent
azure sky above

how many times has the fire burned
transforming
transfiguring
the emotional body?

how many times have I wandered
looking for answers and finding only
more interesting questions

I go to the desert to come home
I go home to find myself
I find myself in the burning embers

in the great fire
my heart is burnished
brushed
and burned clean

in the great fire
I fall in love again
only this time
I am awake
and the azure sky is as transparent as my imagination

Mark Jan Wlodarkiewicz

Reflecting on an Image

I am dropping down to find something I thought I had lost, only to realize en masse, that I had only now just discovered a new form of beauty. Multiple split-second decisions lead me to believe that it might be captured on film, or in print, perhaps even on tape or post-event conversations, but that's purely a residual fraction, burned into a now collective memory — individual experiences becoming part of the overall community, countlessly layering energy to create this entity. I find myself, sometimes desperately, looking for a similar daily view. Just to see something remotely familiar — catch a glimpse of what I hope is to come, and for how I hope to be. I know I must wait for a return to a happier place, and unmotivated anxiety sets in ... circles of mania taking hold ... breathe the thing in ... breathe the thing out ... optimism for a formerly pessimistic curmudgeon has come in the form of devout appreciation of all the wondrous reasons behind the creative life that forms into and becomes Burning Man.

d6

The Playa
(Black Rock Desert)

Open and stretching

Inviting me into everywhere.

Like that cracked Earth,

My heart opens ... to hold

The immense blue above

And all that is beyond,

Unseen but forever there.

Forgetting in that moment,

That somewhere in time

It will need to bleed.

Michael Tscheu

from **creations**

did you stop and watch the sunset?

did you watch the sky change color?

did you watch the mountains turned into cardboard

cutouts

into caricatures of themselves

did you watch this happen?

did you see this

slowly happen?

Michael Peter Magoski

Forget not that the earth delights to feel your bare feet
and the winds long to play with your hair

— Kahlil Gibran

stepping out of a white light dome Blaze spins away

below the quilt of stars winking at the playa's players;

she spins and spins with turquoise sarong dancing in the wind, its

dolphins jumping in and out of the Nevada nightwaves;

locks of red knot around her head; her eyes catch sight of

bouncing kangaroos passing by as she spins until dizziness

draws her back into the bright white light spilling trance

into the playa's hands

Bonnie Schneider (bonnieblaze)

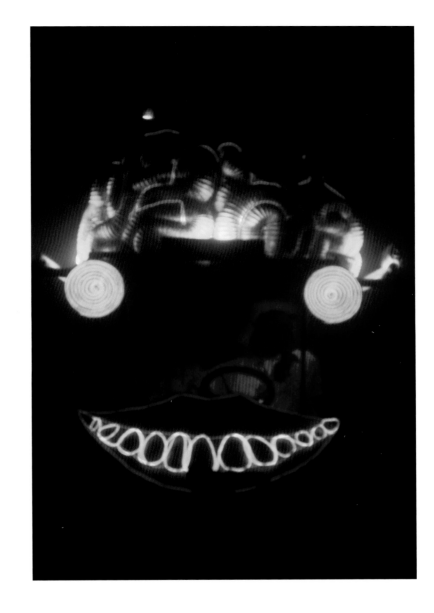

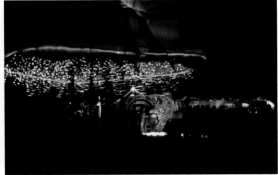

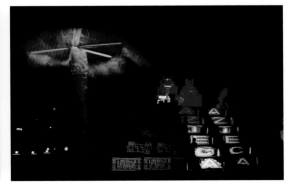

Somebody Put Out Camron

It was time, they said. Burn night was here. Drumming and chanting filled the air, the sun was sinking below the horizon, and the shadows were growing longer. I wanted this night to mean nothing, to have no significance, no risk. But now, that was impossible. I donned a golden mask and set out for the burn circle. Inside, the Man glistened. Earlier, he and I had said goodbye. "See you soon," Camron said, confronting my growing anxiety with an expression of confidence. That afternoon, I had attempted to curb my fears by encircling the fire cannons with a white protective glow when a passerby stopped, proclaiming: "You're like an angel." I snapped out of this state, realizing I'd been discovered in my private ritual.

Right then, the five cannons of *The Impotence Compensation Project* were on their way to the burn circle where, after dark, they would blast fireballs of kerosene hundreds of feet into the blackened sky. The other cannons would be controlled remotely, but Camron would be handling Bertha, the mother cannon, creating the most powerful spectacle of fire at an entirely pyro-centric event. His job was both heroic and extremely dangerous. Spacemen-like in silver fire suits, the *ICP* crew made their final preparations. I had been assured they rigorously tested everything and had built in numerous safety nets. Yet, something tugged at me. Not knowing which cannon was Bertha, I feared I had not completed my protective spell earlier. Had I adequately appeased the fire gods with my novice charms and spells?

I rested all hope on the talisman we had brought to the playa, an eight-inch toy giraffe with a rabbit's foot for a head — a present for Camron's birthday. He had employed this objet d'art turned good luck charm back home in San Francisco to oversee the packing of the Disturbia truck. Upon the Lucky Giraffe I had bestowed the powers of a divine entity, but my reverence for this holy piece of plastic and fur was quickly mocked. On the first day on the playa, I was flipping the air mattress and slightly bumped Giraffe's resting place on the cooler. Plop! Off came the foot, or, um, head. Utterly spooked, I hid Giraffe in a paper bag and snuck past Camron, who was engrossed with Bertha, to seek out a glue gun. The rabbit's foot held, but not for long. The heat and dust quickly rendered the glue useless. Again, a slight move to Giraffe and — plop! — Its head fell off again. "Mwaha-ha! The outcome has already been decided, foolish girl!" the red rabbit fur seemed to say, even as it dangled from

the Giraffe's neck by no more than a gummy piece of nearly dried glue. One last repair job and the rabbit's foot seemed to hold. It was coming with me into the circle.

Nearing burn time, the hum of the crowd increased, as did the requests for booze and smokes, and the number of rangers blockading between the thickening crowd and the Man. Even Giraffe seemed to be in good form, attracting the attention of a nearby photographer. The moon itself, aglow with a fiery orange hue, rose from the dusky mountains embracing the playa. With the omnipresent dust and wind now long gone, in that welcome stillness, all were focused on the circle. The overwhelming cause for celebration and the magnificence of nature's compliance negated the superstitious undercurrents that had earlier plagued me.

Then it began.

Geysers spewing fat columns of flame and smoke trails rent the air above, one, then another and another. The fire fountains were set to the beat of Orff's *Carmina Burana*. It was hot, scorching hot. The light and heat consumed me, my previous fears suspended in awe. After one large blast from old Bertha, however, I saw a small fire begin to creep over a kerosene splashed cannon. Something had gone wrong. Panic set in. My body seemed to propel itself upward, as if gravity suddenly didn't matter. But a moment later, the small fire subsided, and seeing that Camron was okay, the laws of physics took over again and pulled me back to the Playa. The performance resumed. In unison, all five cannons sang out, including Bertha, spouting higher and more intensely than before. The heat and volume of flame seemed so close, several people scurried away.

And the Man burned. As the crowd rushed toward the embers I moved across the burn circle, covered in the golden mask, holding Giraffe above me. Distinguishable in his silver suit was a very sooty Camron. With my heartbeat and breath now back to normal, I expressed thanks to the giraffe for a job well done — and acknowledged the forces of chaos that added to the evening's drama. Totally nonplussed, he joked about being on fire for a few seconds before *ICP* co-creator Alexander Rose made the kind request: "Somebody put out Camron." It's a punchline that will certainly be used for years to come. 🔥

Jennifer C. Clemente

The Flight to Mars

Since you cannot resist galactic creatures, warp pirates, flaming meteors or swanky starcraft, you have decided to take the *Flight to Mars*. You walk through the gate, and follow the arrow to the right. As you proceed into the mouth of a space monster, a ramp in the foreground carries Burning Man in a coaster car past an erupting volcano. The monster's razor-sharp fangs carry a message politely reminding you not to smoke for your own safety.

Soon you are in the Computer Control Room. Input devices and oscilloscopes abound, indicating that all glowing circuits are functioning perfectly. From there, you enter the Airlock. Blinking control panels inform you of a complete system overload, and you're ejected into the Stratosphere. It's cloudy and confusing, but you're a great pilot and you know the way. Before long, you're in the entrance to the Gland Canyon, the psychedelic wormhole shortcut to Mars. Blue lights swirl and strobe around you, directing you to its apex. You enter the Ice Caves, and the color temperature shifts to a more Martian quality. Stalagmites and stalactites paw at you as you pass through. You enter an orange nebula, and the soft textures beckon you: "touch me, feel me."

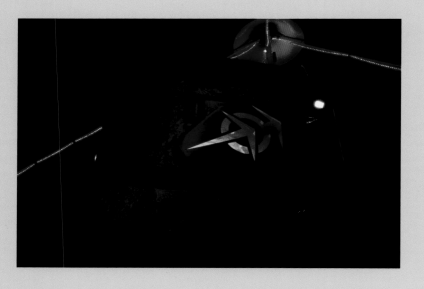

Alas, you near the end of your flight, but the adventure has only begun. You must be reborn as a Martian, and penetrate the giant vagina into the Birthing Box to know the planet Mars. Traveling back through what seems like the same type of port-hole that originally deposited you on Earth, you find an inner world, where there is life and all manner of spaced-out magnificent artifacts. Greeting you are many wild, ecstatic creatures, dancing about, having a good fuckin' time and ready to tell you how beautiful you are. You're in an alien metropolis of nanotech rhythms. An enormous Lunar Lander stands before you, and its pilot has only been here a few days, but he's using his remaining supplies to have a housewarming party. There is plenty of intelligent life on this planet, far more than Earth. You can gyrate your atoms or make yourself at home in the lounge. Why would you ever return, except to take the flight again? 🔥

Alex David Wilson, with contributions from Marquita Gomez and Jeff Larson

I Burned You Up

There was a day
    I burned you up.
One day out of a thousand
    others that could have
    called your name
    to a crisp.
    But this one ...
    I chose this one day
    threw you on the fire
    like a pencil breaking
    like a mudflap
        catching mud.

And you were gone.

There was a day
    I chose to let my heart
    be free to love
    be free to catch
    another fire burning.
There was a day.

There was a day
    I burned you up
    and started my own fire
    with gasoline and woodchips
    with gasoline soaked lingerie
    with gasoline to a crisp
        I burned you up.
And it could have been
a thousand other days.
But this one ...
I chose this one day
to throw you on the fire
and you were gone.

Allison Yates

Scene I

My first arrival at Burning Man, and I'm flying across the desert kicking up ribbons of dust. Like Mad Max, but in a Toyota. **In the middle of a dusty nowhere appear rag-tag camps of nomads,** bejeweled art cars, stiletto heels and parasols. High fashion meets low desert. We try to get our bearings in a city without streets, eventually coming to a large orange parachute attached to a circle of RVs. I end the day jumping on a trampoline as a DJ plays the theme from *Star Wars*.

One night while walking back to camp I notice something blinking on the ground, and then another one. I step back and notice more little lights, red lights, spaced out over a large circular area. I'm on an alien landing platform, or in a matrix of LED nodes. My mind takes off before bringing me back to earth. I chuckle at the realization that someone painstakingly planted these dynamic dots in the ground, so subtle that most people probably trod over them obliviously or dismiss them as a trick of the eye.

Scene II

A day later we grab a ride to Trego hot springs to the east of the city, across the train tracks. I've been anticipating and dreading this — the moment of public nudity. I had managed up to that point to avoid it, more out of fear of feeling vulnerable than embarrassment. I linger behind my friends and submerge into the murky liquid without any notice. In the mud my anxiety dissolves. I marvel at the blueness of the water, how it turns us into moving statues. We finger-paint on each other, anointing our skins with a protective coating from the sun. It is playful and innocent. Two women begin playing flutes on the banks of the water. Soon people in the hot springs are passing a violin arm-over-arm across the water to a third and it becomes a trio. Now, uninhibited, I dance behind them as they play their impromptu concert. A train passes by and everyone smiles and waves. It is one of those rare moments when the world stands still, allowing you to consciously absorb it all before it passes on and the sound and motion resume.

Scene III

It is another hot and muggy day. The temperature is so high it bakes the dust into our pores, leaving us caked in layers of grimy sweat. I'm tired of the relentless sun and sit, exhausted, in the shade. All of a sudden a dark, ominous looking cloud appears in the distance. **It hovers in the south, as out of place as a nuclear mushroom.** The energy in the air is palpable, as our excitement over the possibility of rain mingles with the electricity-generating ions above us. In a few minutes the cloud is directly over us and water is pouring down. We scamper to take refuge in an RV but then change our minds, dancing in the rain; purifying our souls. The cloud moves quickly and soon it has sailed on. The rain stops as abruptly as it started, leaving us drip-drying in the warm air. As the activity of the city dies down, a double rainbow appears in the wake of the cloud's path. With audible sighs all around, the city gazes up at the arc positioned perfectly over the Man. 🔥

Elinor Mills Abreu

Love Poem for the Playa

What you never expected was the tenderness
you'd feel for the dust: how you'd relish
the way it stood your hair on end, grow
fond of it lining your bowl and spoon, the rim
of your water bottle. How you'd rub it
between your hands like talcum, lift your head
at the scent of it once you'd arrived
back home.

You didn't know you'd stand in a dust storm —
full moon — and wait for flames to emerge
from a cloud thick as fishermen's fog. You'd bend
to the sound of it, your skin alive with the rush
of a lakebed taking flight.

You couldn't imagine how it would settle
on each thing without discernment: tree legs
twisting into a walking god, flags gone loud
in the wind, a field of improbable sunflowers,
the woman who fed you
leftover curry and rice.

This is what you would take
home with you: a yearning
for something heated, untamed, vast
and inhospitable, and you'd love it
like your own sun rising,
like the matter of your bones.

Brittney Corrigan (Lola)

Shoe Surfing

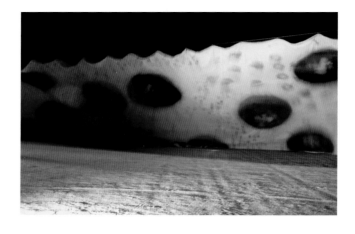

The full moon sits balanced precariously above the mountain-strewn horizon, the impartial judge presiding over this courtroom of chaos. Right now I'm truly content, genuinely, deep-down happy. The reason for my state of elation has nothing to do with artificial forms of stimulation. I'm experiencing a ridiculousness buzz. This is the high associated with activity that is so utterly weird and deviant that no one in their right mind would conceive of it.

And tonight's entertainment definitely fits the weird and deviant bill. I'm perched on a king-size skateboard with big knobby rubber tires, an off-road version of the standard street board toted by mall rats the world over. The wind is whipping around my finely balanced torso, purple robes fluttering wraith-like in my wake. With one hand I'm holding onto a water ski-style tow handle. The other hand is arced backwards for better balance. And the vehicle towing me, tearing across the vast, open playa at 30 mph is a gigantic purple shoe.

Created by my campmates, it's a four-wheeler with a plywood and chicken wire frame, covered in purple fabric and silver trim to form a two-seater shoemobile. It usually tows a sofa behind it, but tonight we're going for speed and agility. Besides, the sofa broke off in an earlier misadventure.

As the shoe makes a sharp left turn I brace myself for the centrifugal forces that swing me and the board way out to the side of the shoe, almost level with it. I wave briefly at the drivers with my balancing hand before being whipped viciously back in line with the shoe as with a sharp snap the rope slack is taken up. This is living. This is what humans were meant to be doing with their spare time and ingenuity: continually developing and refining new forms of entertainment to appease the inner child. Hunter-gatherers were just a necessary step along the evolutionary ladder to homo loco, the lesser-spotted desert freak.

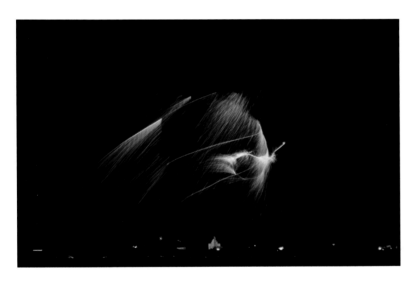

The powerful lure of novelty should never be underestimated. Breaking out of normal modes of thinking is a crucial weapon in the war against mediocrity. Here I am, dressed like a freak in fluttering purple robes and a Mexican wrestler's mask, surfing at high speed behind a shoe under a brilliant full moon on one of the most remote deserts on the planet. It can definitely get more ridiculous than this, but not much.

We fly down the axis of the glowing neon man and head like moths to the brightest light on the playa, the Afterlife. Beams of solid white light arc up into the dusty atmosphere, streaming through the installation's locus in the sky, a circle of iridescent pillars imitating the legendary tunnel of pure light supposedly seen during near-death experiences. Human figures slowly take shape as eerie silhouettes against the piercing white background, resembling the landing scene from *Close Encounters.* As we approach, the shoe starts to veer away and I manipulate the rope for my own close encounter. I recognize a group of friends who built the installation (Radiant Atmospheres), and head for them.

Screaming like a banshee, I close in for the kill. They look around just in time to see the incoming weirdo loco, their eyes registering fleeting astonishment, and then I'm gone, pulling out before impact and leaving a cloud of playa dust in my wake. Onwards and outwards into the void, I cruise towards the otherworldly glow of the moonset, cackling with glee. To me, this is the essence of freedom. The freedom to be ridiculous. 🔥

Jon Ross

Wedding Day

The crowd is very thick now. I hold Pearl's hand tightly, because I don't want to lose her. Her wedding dress sticks to her body like paint and **she would stop traffic anywhere but Burning Man.** I shoot my cuffs; the air has cooled and my dark dinner jacket, white dress shirt, and slender black tie feel entirely appropriate in the cool of the evening.

"Where are the others?" I wonder.

"Who cares," says Pearl. "Let's just get to the front."

She cleaves the crowd with her beauty, and soon we are in the midst of thousands of people under a brilliant dark sky peppered with stars. Ahead of us is the orange glow of the bonfires around The Man. His limbs are neatly outlined by long purple neon lights, like some gaudy Vegas street sign, and there is a clear circle of about fifty yards all around him. I can see Larry Harvey in his Stetson standing on the steps below the Man.

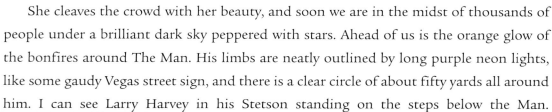

He leans on the steps as though the Playa was his drawing room and the Man was his grand piano. Every now and then he raises his hand to wave, and everyone roars. Silhouetted figures are moving busily about, checking the charges that will eventually ignite the Man. Figures with torches, like something out of a Frankenstein movie, walk around to make sure the crowd stays back. There is some kind of commotion behind us, and we turn. I can see a man's head moving towards us above the crowd. He must be riding on some kind of vehicle, moving at the pace of a stately walk, and it must be a fair size, because the crowd behind us gets

out the way. **He's driving the sofa,** a motorized green three-seater job. A couple of men, naked from the waist up, are sitting on it, and the man I first saw, with a deep tan and a kind, weathered face, is driving. It stops right in front of us, and the two men jump off. **"Thanks man, catch you later,"** says one.

They disappear into the crowd. The sofa itself is empty. Pearl jumps on, smiles at the driver, and I see we're in. I'm too polite, so I have to say "Mind if we join you?"

He looks above our heads at The Man and says, "All aboard." The sofa starts to move. It's nice to be sitting down after walking all day. I can feel the muscles in my back melt into the cushions. The people who moments before were in our way now step neatly aside.

The driver taps my shoulder, and says, "Gin and tonic?" and hands me a large, cold plastic bottle.

"Very nice," says Pearl when she's had a sip.

We press forward, enjoying the looks of surprise and amusement that the sofa creates. People start to shout to those in front to let them know we're coming, with cries of "Make way! Make way for the King and Queen of Burning Man!"

I'm glad I dressed up. Pearl squeezes my hand and says, "I always knew I was an absolute Queen."

Her eyes are shining. We crawl through the crowd until we get to the edge of the circle, and then we stop, and I wait for our driver to kick us out. He

leans forward and says, "Wanna stay and watch the burn?"

We have comfortable, upholstered front row seats, an adoring populace, and a decent gin and tonic. I say, "We should get married everyday." She kisses me hard on the lips, and the Man ignites. 🔥

Michael Parsons

The fire redefines the sky with

heat, ash and glowing embers.

Its towering wall draws us near

as it screams at the hailing night.

helen13

A Haiku

Tell it to the Man.

He stands tall against the sky.

Oh, wait! We burned Him!

Sadie Damascus

from **Leaving Black Rock**

what you sacrifice must be beautiful, the barter

must be meaningful you cannot trade a few used D-batteries

for the silk slip someone loved her in

you cannot trade a short shabby wicker man

for all of your ills purged on this playa, you need something

bigger than mile after mile of clean slate bone white clay,

salt that leaves its signature in cracks, little hexagons

of alkaline, silicates of soil taking their place in ordered chaos

telling you what it is in its breaking apart

(gypsum in your pores after three days of salt walking

parched skin like your arizona grandma's bare heels

torn and feathered at the back)

the fissures map the way in,

unravel the seamstress' jagged pattern

someone was born here at dawn

Eilish Nagle

Mausoleum

The priests of high weirdness, denizens of Whatever, stand atop our buzz observation tower watching the sun sink behind the mountains as the full moon slowly pokes its grinning head above the opposing mountain range. The whole city erupts in feral wolf howls to greet the gleaming satellite into our plane of existence. Sunday night at Burning Man. I've been saving myself all week. Tonight is my night for serious mayhem.

From the tower I can see some action on the other side of Gigsville, looking suspiciously like the Skynyrd camp barbecue. My senses do not deceive me. We eat, drink and are generally very merry around the *Car-B-Q* while the Skynyrd band behaves badly (vomiting mid-song, abusing goats, etc.) until it begins to get dark, at which time the Sindicate girls take to the Gigsville stage with their outrageous cabaret routine, in a Moulin Rouge-meets-Madonna dance style. My home village, in which I've spent ridiculously little time this year, is going off before it returns to an insignificant patch of dusty playa in the middle of a barren desert. This is the way of Burning Man. **Beauty is only temporary in this environment.**

After some preparation time (retrieving goggles, dust mask and fireproof nomex jumpsuit), I set off for the Esplanade. A crowd is gathering outside Dr. Megavolt's setup at the Sindicate. Matty the Mutaytor, an incredible drummer, has his drum kit inside a large chicken wire cage right next to the imposing bulk of a 10-foot Tesla coil. Girls are go-go dancing in cages nearby. Dr. Megavolt is dancing around in his wire mesh suit, directing the million-volt plasma arcs over the various cages as the Mutaytor keeps the rhythm a-movin' and a-groovin'. Excellent fucko entertainment, but I have an important date to keep.

Cycling away from the Esplanade and out onto the open playa, the wind picks up and a whiteout envelops me as heavy gusts liberate sheets of loose desert floor and launch them swirling through the air, wrapping everything in a dense white blanket. The full moon projects a ghostly glow, lighting the whiteout from within, creating an eerie incandescent fog which twists and swirls and chokes and blinds. To all intents and purposes I am deaf and blind. Shrouded shapes loom out of the mist and seconds later dissipate in my wake.

Glowing vehicles, buses packed with people, fire-breathing behemoths, all appear and disappear like magic — soundless, perfect moments from a bizarre dream. Big yellow cat vans with bright headlight eyes, glowing neon fish tractors, armored school buses with marching bands atop, a disco truck, a missile car, land yachts, people on stilts, people on fucked-up blinking bikes, in every kind of attire imaginable, clutching rags and dust masks to their mouths and noses, trying vainly to protect their already playa-tainted lungs. The memory of this magical cycle ride will live with me forever. I can imagine this being the scene outside Kubla Kahn's pleasure dome as the tribes converge to gain entrance to the paradise within, an oasis in the harsh desert terrain of Xanadu.

The feeling around the Mausoleum is intense. This is not just another big fire, but something so much more. The emotional energy poured into this creation is unbelievable. Many separate groups of friends who walked into the Mausoleum during the day confessed to bursting into tears from the power trapped in the towering edifice. **The collective grief of a whole city, entombed in its most beautiful structure, ready for release by fire.**

The only problem is no one can see the Mausoleum through the pea-soup whiteout. The burn ends up delayed for around an hour while we wait for the storm to abate. During this time I wander around, staring at all the faces and vehicles crowded around, like the freaks convention this so obviously is. This is my tribe. These are my people. Folk who devote their time, energy and power to being out in the middle of a desert in the middle of nowhere in the middle of a dust storm to witness a gigantic intricate temple burn to the ground. Freaks, weirdos, adventuresome souls. My brothers and sisters. My kin. Only the hardcore need apply.

Suddenly the wind abates, and the Mausoleum structure looms out of the haze, back-lit in glowing red from its afterlife tower. Fire starts to lick at the base, and quickly jumps up the insides until the whole glorious temple is ablaze, consuming the city's grief as it combusts into carbon dioxide and ash and memories. There is no screaming or cheering, just awe-struck faces illuminated by the glowing pyre, jeweled tears tracing their hesitant path down many a dusty cheek. As the temple collapses in on itself, the end of the funeral is marked, energy is released and cheers go up — the tribe rushes in to sing and dance around the remaining superheated pile of flaming wood, pools of flame licking towards La Luna, the over-seeing Lady of the dance.

Tension and release. The oldest trick in the book for generating a great performance, drawing us up tight with emotion, filling our hearts with pain and pleasure, then torching the pressure with ritual until we are cleansed, and can continue afresh — lighter, transformed, absolved.

Following the incandescent red glow burning through the dense airborne particle mist, I make my way to the *Afterlife*, an immense lighting structure pumping out 50,000 watts of photon power into the sky, illuminating the surrounding area like daylight as the beams hit billions of dust particles and reflect their energy back to ground-zero on the playa below. My favorite installation on the playa, usually somber and otherworldly, tonight they're having an after party with dance music, and playing the lighting tower like a disco.

In the meantime, however, the dust storm is back with a vengeance, and conditions are tough to survive. The Black Rock Mobile Library pulls up out of the mist, so in I pop to browse the shelves. It's at this point the ridiculousness of the situation hits me. Here I am in a library in a bus in the middle of a dust storm on a harsh desert in an extremely unpopulated area of the western United States, 6,000 miles from where I come from. Outside, my friends are having a rave with the best lighting gear any club will ever see and preparing to fire off a huge flame cannon. Surreal doesn't even begin to describe this situation. How do you explain stuff like this to people who've never been? If this isn't truly living life as it was meant to be led, I have no idea what is.

Suddenly the serenity of the library bus is shattered by loud bangs and crackles. I rush out, and in the distance the *Pyromid* is going off amid a blaze of twinkling fireworks. Missed it. Oh well. Fiery fun to be had out here, too. Mr. Foo has set up Betsy, his homemade flame cannon (homemade — as if you can buy these in the shops). It's a small, innocuous piece of precision engineering that charges up a closed tube with 150 psi of nitrogen, fills up a second, open-ended tube with half a gallon of gasoline and upon the trigger of a remote switch, releases a valve between the tubes, propelling the gasoline out of the nozzle on top and through a propane ignition ring. This causes a 50-foot fireball to go searing up into the sky. Impressive. Fun. Genius. From a very early age I've been hypnotized by fire, and tonight is no exception. Watching red, black and yellow clouds exploding from within, billowing in chaotic globular waves, radiating intense heat and lighting up the playa for hundreds of yards all around, I am rooted to the spot. My mind is no longer under my control — it is the fire interfacing directly with my reptilian brain, programming my mind with unknown instructions.

As the Foo show comes to a close, I decide to remove my presence from the dust (which is mainly blowing along the central boulevard from Center Camp out to where the Man used to stand). I hurtle across the playa (holding onto the Nurse and Dodger's golf cart for propulsion), and quickly arrive back at the city just in time to see huge plumes of liquid flame scorching their way horizontally across the open playa.

The *Vegematic of the Apocalypse* is in action. A twisted, demented, thoroughly evil-looking vehicle wrought from iron, looking like a cross between a medieval war device and a high-tech penny-farthing. Its central iron tube spurts a stream of high-pressure fuel, torching anything that dares get in its way, while its passengers pedal to propel it upon its roving pyro adventures. Then an unmistakable noise permeates the night, ripping the atmosphere into purple-glowing ionized shreds — a large Tesla coil going off nearby. Not Dr. Megavolt, but another coil, rigged with the big iron moth vehicle next to it. A human figure encased in a metal cage hangs from a huge cherry-picker crane, swinging back and forth through the arcing of the Tesla. If this isn't art, I don't know what is.

After an age of watching the Tesla, I notice a lot of art cars gathering around Michael Christian's Dali-esque headless beast structure, so I head over to see what weirdness is being concocted over there. I soon notice that a large cherry picker has lifted Mr Foo up to the top of the tall, spindly, fragile-looking sculpture, where he is installing his flame cannon inside. One-hundred percent ridiculous, completely stupid and utterly over the top. Perfect. As a finale they're going to make the sculpture belch clouds of fiery plasma into the dawn sky. Salvador himself would be proud. The expectant atmosphere is awesome — this is living like kings! However, after a few hours and some false starts, it appears there's an issue with the fuel pump. The system is firing properly, but has no fuel to fire. A disappointment to all, and an anticlimax to the evening — but when art and engineering interface, there's always a high probability of failure. That the idea was conceived and nearly executed pays tribute to the absolute genius one can witness at Burning Man.

Burning Man may have changed character over the years, but it's still the weirdest, most intense crucible of creative energy and beauty on the Earth. And until it stops being so, I'll be there coating the inside of my lungs with playa dust every Labor Day weekend. 🔥

Jon Ross

Being a partial list of (physical) things found at Burning Man:

One red pipe cleaner — shaped into an irregular loop.

Two pop-out nozzles from water bottles — hate them myself. The natural flow of water is so much more beautiful.

Many cigarette butts — How can so many people be so clueless as to drop them? Or, how can it matter so much more here?

A blue horn — fallen from the head of an azure satyr, who was bummed, until he met the previous owner of a red horn,

   the she-imp who no doubt plucked and dropped it in a show of passion and eternal bonding.

An unused yellow tent peg — absolutely irresistible.

One bicycle spoke reflector — very sparkly. We like it.

A card from the Limbo Lounge, number 1821.

One silk scarf (which I am wearing) — found at the ashes of the Man in this morning's dawn.

Ron Meiners
September 7, 1998, Black Rock

Tribal Artifacts and the People Who Love Them:
Notes on the Art of Burning Man

by Mark Van Proyen

The past four decades form a distinctive chapter in the history of American art. This was the era of the National Endowment of the Arts (NEA), a much-maligned federal agency established a few short weeks after the Gulf of Tonkin Resolution set in motion the Vietnam War in 1964. In 1989, Senator Jesse Helms excoriated this agency for its support of allegedly obscene art, ironically enough, just a few months before the fall of the Berlin Wall.

Federal support of the arts and the final chapter of the Cold War was reflected in the cold attributes of the art authorized and professionalized by the NEA: the flat, crisply impersonal iconography of Pop Art; the gleaming, antiseptic surfaces of Minimalist sculpture; and the extreme psychological remove evidenced by the activities routinely gathered under Conceptual Art.

In retrospect, we can fairly say the art spawned by these movements was representative of an ethos of art for bureaucracy's sake — they all self-consciously presumed to take their place quickly on the icy white walls of the contemporary art museum. Thus, they exhibited only slight regard for the possibility that art might have other kinds of work to do in a larger and more complicated social world.

In the context of the bureaucratic and academic art world of the past forty years, artworks in the modes of Pop, Minimalism and Conceptualism make a kind of perfect sense — they reflect and embody the hyper-quantified modes of statistical valuing intrinsic to large institutions of every type. Therefore, they can all be seen as tribal artifacts, as much the prisoners of their own isolated contexts and protocols as African Masks or Hopi Kachinas are of the specific ceremonial aspects of their original use. This realization prompts an obvious question: what if the context for making and viewing contemporary art was radically altered and/or removed from the moieties of institutional existence?

To its enduring credit, Burning Man has not only asked this very question, but has forced it as an important issue in the ongoing debate about the character and value of contemporary art. Perfect timing; as history shows, the 1990s were earmarked by a massive consolidation of corporate control of the arts, working under the guise of an interna-tional industry — cultural tourism. The unprecedented boom in the building of new museums, as well as a proliferation of international biennial-type exhibitions taking place around the globe proved this undeniable fact. Part and parcel with this consolidation, we witnessed the transformation of the NEA into an even more bureaucratized shadow of its former self, evolving into an agency that by statute could no longer give any money directly to artists.

As euphoria over the Cold War's end gave way to the omnipresent chill of New Globalism, it became increasingly clear artists would have to adopt a radical do-it-yourself ethic if they hoped to keep their work from being reduced to a corporate advertisement or the visual equivalent of a bureaucratic white paper. The 1990s created unprecedented possibilities for doing exactly that. With the massive proliferation of the Internet came the possibility for grass roots organizing, extending beyond geographic limitations. Never was there a time so ripe for the aggressive advancement of what Andre Malraux prophesied as a museum without walls. And now, over a full decade after Burning Man's fateful beginning, the artistic results are speaking for themselves.

Nineteen-ninety-seven was a particularly good year for large-scale sculpture at Burning Man. In Jim Mason's *Temporal Decomposition*, time literally stood still. The piece — a monumental ice ball suffused with broken clocks, illuminated by the flame of a propane torch implanted at its crown — was completely constructed in the desert's arid environment. It took almost a full week to melt, aided by Burning Man participants encouraged to use its surface as a convenient aid for cooling overheated skin.

Michael Christian's *Bone Arch* was a stupendous memorial to the harshness of the desert and the sense of mortality bred by it. Made of hundreds of bleached cattle bones affixed to a steel frame, the tower itself resembled a giant bone, a monumental vertebra or pelvic girdle, reminding the participant of the failed cattle ranches hosted nearby. Christian's work, *Flock*, made an impressive showing at Burning Man 2001. This stunningly ambitious work — intermingled vines of twisted metal rods — featured the subtle morphological transformation from plant to animal shapes.

Underlit by green lights, the figure stretched 40 feet high and swayed in the wind like a giant stalk of surreal kelp affixed to the bottom of some post-apocalyptic lake.

In 1998, several works stood out. Finley Fryer's *Plastic Chapel* was an elaborate three-story theatrical stage made of over 27,000 recycled plastic toys. Internal illumination made it glow at night like stained glass, an eerie apparition in the vast desert. The Chapel hosted many performances. Michael Peppe performed a segment of his *Behaviourmusik* titled *Information White-Out*, featuring the artist precisely mimicking a barrage of media messages at high speed. That same year, Fryer constructed a giant Rubik's Cube, and the year after, a tall sentinel figure with a diver's helmet, also created from discarded plastic.

Wit and sophistication were revealed by Steven Raspa's *Sacred Grove & Wheel of Faith*. It occupied an acre of empty desert bisected into four quadrants with corridors of artificial ficus trees sporting large banners at each end: Hope, Pray, Wish, Dream (typical prayers uttered by gamblers). The color and typeface of these words resembled the California State Lottery graphics (a good joke in casino-friendly Nevada). A devotional altar in the form of a roulette wheel resided in the center. The whole installation seemed an elaborate prayer altar reconfigured as a cosmic observatory à la Stonehenge.

In 1999, Steve Heck created a Piano Boat out of discarded pianos and television sets, a surreal tramp steamer sailing away from the city out to the desert horizon. Closer to the city was another boat of sorts, Andy Hill's the *H.M.S. Love*, a wood reproduction of a bow and conning tower of a surfacing submarine. Like

Fryer's Chapel, the Love doubled as a performance platform for skateboarders, musicians and DJs alike — another example of how artwork can function as a multi-tasking object.

The construction of the semi-circular layout of Black Rock City in 2000 was spectacularly enhanced by the *Beaming Man* installation. Created by Russell Wilcox and team, it used lasers on 20-foot-tall towers to articulate the Vitruvian Burning Man logo from one end of the two-mile-wide city to the other; viewable in its entirety only from

a high altitude. Located near city center were two monumental works addressing that year's theme (The Body): *Body of Knowledge*, by Dana Albany, and *The Faces of Man*, by Dan Das Mann. The former was a monumentally scaled figure comprised of hundreds of books glued together, poetically suggesting we're all the sum of the wisdom we acquire. Faces was a trio of 20-foot-tall masks made of various materials, surrounding a central core, with one actually crying tears of fire at night.

The four-story *Temple of Tears* was far and away the most impressive work at Burning Man 2001. An ambitious and bizarre hybrid of Balinese, Tibetan and Gothic influences, this plywood mausoleum

(created by David Best, Jack Haye and scores of volunteers) featured an astounding amount of filigreed ornament obsessively applied in many overlapping layers. The layers were constructed out of the plywood remnants from a toy dinosaur skeleton factory. Casting a somber shadow over the otherwise obstreperous festivities, the *Temple of Tears* acted as a site of remembrance for lost comrades. Inside were hundreds of written eulogies left by event participants, ceremonially burned with the temple amidst a nocturnal sandstorm the final night of that year's event, inspiring a mood of reverential introspection.

What is common to all of these works is their openness and availability to many different kinds and types of audience involvement. Oftentimes, they can be looked at, played with and/or performed upon and almost always they convene communal participation around them. Aesthetically and symbolically, many of them address themselves to the ideas of warmth and regeneration, forming a striking contrast to the aesthetics of cold strategy so often featured in institutional settings. Even their desert home emphasizes itself as a place of extreme heat, perhaps even being the kind of heat that might inspire passion and prophesy. And springing from this heated involvement comes the important question: if it's possible to create such grand things in such an inhospitable environment, then why can't they be created everywhere? It's a question well worth asking. ◓

— This essay is an updated adaptation of a lecture of the same title given by the author at the San Francisco Public Library on August 6, 1998.

Seven years ago, **Dana Albany** was studying biology with aspirations of becoming a scientist. After attending Burning Man for the first time in 1994, she volunteered to help build the large wooden neon effigy known as The Man. She built her first solo sculpture, a camel, in 1996. In 1999, she built the *Bone Tree*, a 27-foot mobile structure comprised of bones collected from nearby ranches and covered in spot lighting. In 2000, the year Burning Man based its theme on the body, Dana created a sculpture of a man composed of discarded books: *The Body of Knowledge*. Its burning evoked the destruction of the great library of Alexandria. Dana was supported and assisted on all projects by Flash Hopkins.

Stephanie Andrews, aka StephStuph, is the creator of *The Hall of Possible Selves*, a meditation on identity made from Plexiglas, photographic transparency and Mylar encapsulated in columns of light. Paul Jordan helped with the original construction of the installation, which was featured at the six o'clock position on The Wheel of Time in 1999 and in Firetown camp in 2000. Stephanie, a Burner since 1997, was the head organizer of the Crystal Palace Costume Ball in 2001. Previously a technical director at Pixar, she is pursuing her M.F.A. at the Art Institute of Chicago and continuing to integrate science, technology and cinema into her artwork.

ANTENNA was founded in 1980 by Artistic Director Chris Hardman, and has been producing site-specific events and spectacles around the Bay Area for 18 years. For Burning Man 2000 the group created the *Sands of Time* exhibit, an interactive project that blended science, art, history and popular culture to examine the meaning of the new Millennium. The piece was a 35-minute journey through the history of the universe, from the Big Bang to present day, sculpted in sand. Participants wore headphones and listened to music, voices and sound effects as they walked through this performance sculpture, designed to resemble a gigantic Zen Garden. The history of the universe consumed five football fields of desert, whereas the past 2,000 years was represented by one grain of sand.

Neal Borowsky, aka Steel Neal, aka The Future Primitive, created *The Agony of Man*. Three times the size of a human and weighing over 1,200 pounds, it took two years to construct and debuted in 1997. It was built for a performance piece titled *The Future Primitive*, which portrays the last man on a post-apocalypse Earth building the sculpture as his monument to "all the pain and suffering humanity has inflicted upon itself for as long as we have been able to think." In 1999, Neal took the exhibit to Madison Square Garden,

mounting the sculpture on a taxicab chassis and pulling it himself in the Fringe Festival Parade. Neal, who supports himself by making custom metal furniture, has also submitted *The Agony of Man* as a candidate for the World Trade Center Memorial.

A long time ago, **Larry Breed,** aka Ember, pioneered computer graphics applications on a room-filling vacuum-tube computer. In 1995, he showed up on the playa with a truck full of tools to refurbish lampposts, and in 1996, he built the prototype trash fence: a mile-long line of light plastic mesh and bamboo poles. In 1997, Larry constructed the *Spiral Solar Mirror*, a fresnel parabolic reflector that lit the torch of the Naked Fire Goddess. In 1999, recalling a novelty clock escapement from a science-museum exhibit he saw in his childhood, Larry installed *The Chaotick*, an 18-foot self-actuating flaming tetherball that returned in 2000 and 2001. Larry is also an Earth Guardian and DPW volunteer, and proofreads Burning Man newsletters and the *Black Rock Gazette*.

The Cataclysmic Megashear Ranch describes itself as "a collective howl of dissent against the status quo." The name of this San Francisco artists' collective describes the collision of two plates of the Earth's crust, and the ensuing release of enormous energy: a single momentous event spawning thousands of smaller ones. Souls from all walks of life live and work together as one at the ranch, with the common goals of radical self-expression, discovery, creation, destruction, absurdity and anarchy.

Michael Christian is a sculptor from Texas who has lived in the Bay Area for the last seven years. His hobbies include working with sharp objects, pointed sticks, flaming projectiles and fluids that are difficult to remove from clothing. He has been building commissioned works in the desert for the last five years using everything from bones to plastic wrap. His favorite piece is a 16-foot high, 22-foot wide metal pipe organ tree complete with hand pumps to play notes on. His work includes: *The Bone Arch* (1997), with help from Dana Albany, Zach Coffin and Todd Curtis; *Nebulous Entity* (1998), with Christina Harbridge, Lorianne Huft, Todd Curtis, Jay Kravitz, Chaos Kitty, Aron Wolf Baum on sound, David Andres on engineering, Jeremy Lutes on lighting, among many others; *Orbit* (1999), with Christina Harbridge, Jeremy Lutes, David Andres; *Babel* (2000), popularly know as *The Pipe Organ*, with Dave Murphy, Christina Harbridge and Jeremy Lutes; and *Flock* (2001), with Dave Gardner, Michael Bradford, Yael Braha, Austin Cable, Christina Harbridge, Jay Kravitz and Jeremy Lutes.

Dan Das Mann was born in the Andes Mountains to a small tribe called the Mumbatou Nation. He moved to San Francisco and founded Headless Point Studios and Dan Das Mann Studios. Dan has worked with many hundreds of artists and creators on various large-scale installations over the past six years. Special appreciation goes to Danya Parkinson, Larry Lowell, Jeremy Batdorf and Dusty for their work on the *Faces of Man* in 2000 and Philip Bonham, Zeffron and Brian Doherty for their work on the *One Tree* in 1998.

Death Guild is a San Francisco Goth/Industrial nightclub founded in 1993 by David King. It is a community of artists, freaks, gear heads, machinists, survivalists, tech geeks, hillbillies, fire dancers and leather-clad bouncers, all of them wearing big boots. David and friends attended Burning Man for a few years before deciding that Black Rock City was missing something: what good is a city without the wrong side of the tracks? In January 1999, David proposed The Death Guild/Thunderdome Project to a group of about 30 friends. Nine months later, the Dome was erected on the playa, harnesses were strung up and senseless voluntary beatings began. They raced around on rat bikes and stripped-down cars, raising hair on a lot of necks. Death Guild quickly became the bad kids of Black Rock City. Which was exactly what they set out to do.

A resourceful team of friends and fans of numerous persuasions, under the umbrella of **Dragon Debris,** was responsible for 2001's Azteca/Golf of Mexico, a seven-hole mini-golf course themed on an ancient culture. They also created *Pulse* in 2000 and Camp Carnival/Time Flies in 1999. Before Burning Man, they poured all excess creative energies into costume parties and Halloween.

Emerald City (First Landing), a laser-projecting construction based on L. Frank Baum's *Wizard of Oz*, was built on the playa in both 2000 and 2001. The crew includes Stephanie Sutton (Dorothy), Patrick Flanagan (Oz), Randy Johnson (LaserRandy), Allan Lundell (scarecrow and videographer), Sun McNamee (witch and technical cyberchic) and many more munchkins too numerous to mention.

Fandango is a village of several hundred individuals bound together by their inability to submit to a common theme. Each member of Fandango brings his or her own creative idea to the playa, with projects including the Alien Crash Site Bar, the *Glockenspiel* and the Motown Grass Dome. In just over a decade, Fandango has grown from two tents to a theme camp to a village. The name began as simply something to shout to gather the camp's attention on the playa, but ended up saving lives in dust storms and serving as a totemic rallying cry for the Burn.

The Flaming Lotus Girls is a loose-knit collective of female fire artists aged between 10 and 60 who came together in 2000 to create the Flaming Lotus fire cannon. As participants interact with the devices, they also interact with their fellow participants to create an organic sequence of flames. For Burning Man 2002 they are creating the fire fan, a six-barrel kerosene fire cannon with 50-foot flames controlled by a MIDI sequencer and fifty additional propane, kerosene and naptha flowers.

Freezing Man was born out of a desire to bring to Burning Man something that would be truly unique and welcomed by overheated Playans. After abandoning the idea of building a public swimming pool, San Francisco computer programmer and DJ Mike Wertheim decided to bring ice cream to the desert instead. He bought a truck, previously owned by a beer distributor, and turned to his friends to help him make it playa-ready. Michael Lazar designed and built an insulated polyurethane freezer box that used dry ice to keep the treats colder than 30 degrees Fahrenheit. Rus Maxham equipped it with a sound system and speakers. Jon Drukman, Jeff Taylor, Cory West and Mark Camp wrote electronic music to be played as the truck made its rounds. Lisa Seaman designed the colorful, wacky cartoon graphics that decorated the outside. The truck drove the streets of Burning Man in 1998, 1999 and 2000, with volunteers handing out everything from drumsticks to popsicles and ice cream sandwiches to the eager crowds. Sporting dancers and a couch on the roof, the truck passed on-site Nevada health inspections with flying colors every year.

During the past 25 years **Finley Fryer** has created a diverse body of work that includes sculpture, painting and film-making. In 1998, he created the *Plastic Chapel*, an architectural sculpture constructed largely of recycled plastic. The *Plastic Chapel*, aka the *Chapel of the Burning Book* and *The Taj*, was created in collaboration with a group of friends and artists in Dunsmuir, Calif. It was both a monumental and intimate creation lit from within at night, glowing like a giant cube of stained glass. In 1999, Fryer brought to the playa an 18-foot figurative sculpture of a deep sea diver — *Stan the Submerging Man* — accompanied by an audio track created by Bay Area artist Kirk Leclaire. Stan was made of plastic and colored records, and was also illuminated from within at night. In 2000, Fryer created *Coalita*, a fusible glass female figure filled with charcoal and Coca Cola. In 2001, the *Plastic Chapel* returned to the playa as part of the Seven Ages theme.

Charles A. Gadeken has made more than 25 large-scale works of art during his 10 years at Burning Man. For his Illumination Project he has created and destroyed over 500,000 square feet of painted imagery. In 2001, *Illumination Project #18* extended the length of six football fields with 160,000 square feet of painted canvas, 1,500 feet of steel cable and 1,000 lbs. of rigging. Charles started the Illumination Village in 1996 and watched it grow to over 300 people from 16 countries in 2001. His art has been installed at the S-Mova Visual Art Museum in Santa Rosa, Calif., Treasure Island in San Francisco and San Jose's American Music Festival. Charles is the Director of QBOX, a non-profit arts organizations focused on the creation, presentation, discussion and preservation of mechanical, kinetic and electronic art in the Bay Area.

Architect **Rod Garrett** was raised in southern California in the San Fernando Valley. He arrived in the Bay Area during the early '60's in time to encounter the Beat culture of San Francisco, where he became friends with poet Gary Snyder and comic Lenny Bruce. He also taught himself landscape design and became a licensed contractor. In 1995, he attended his first Burning Man and joined the project as chief designer in 1997. Working in collaboration with Larry Harvey, Will Roger, Harley Dubois and other staff members, Rod plans the design of Black Rock City every year. He devised the huge tensiometric structure that houses the community's central café and configured the giant *Laser Man* in 2000. In 2001, he designed the *Temple of Enlightenment* that formed the pedestal of Burning Man.

Jenne Giles drove out of Texas to Burning Man in 1999 and has not been home since. Jenne conceived and constructed the *Ribcage/Birdcage* with collaborator Philip Bonham for Burning Man 2000. In 2001, she built the *Mandala*. Now she is a struggling but happy installation and performance artist in the Bay Area. Jenne gives special thanks to Iaian McAusland, Brian Doherty, Flash, Duncan McColl, Eveline Darroch and Paul Troutman for their immeasurable assistance in accomplishing the improbable.

Christina Harbridge inspires love, camaraderie and no small amount of awe in those fortunate enough to cross paths with her. A businesswoman capable of coaxing humanity away from grim bankers and avaricious attorneys, Christina has been psychic wet nurse and psychedelic den mom to dozens of artist, writers and other dysfunctionals in both the desert and the city. In 1997, sporting a hot-pink Barbie-mobile and pink and white wigs, panties and go-go boots, Christina and Lorianne Huft, or Pinkie and Francie, held one of the most widely attended weddings at Burning Man.

Carl Heiney joined the Detroit Cacophony Society after returning from Burning Man in 1997. In 1999, he built the *Lamp Mobile*, a 25-foot Calderesque piece, created to share a vision he saw of floating table lamps in his home in Detroit. The mobile was designed over many months and constructed in a week with welding assistance from Jeff Evarts. When oil lamps failed in the high winds of the desert, Carl improvised and fashioned flashlights and reflectors for night illumination. He moved to San Francisco in late 1999.

Burning Man 1995 was the first for **Hemi** and **Red** (aka Mitenniloc Amalgamated Incorporated delivering Ambiance and Style at No Cost To You!) and they haven't looked back. They are two founding members of The Illumination Project and the Village. Hemi (Tim) and Red (Colinne) make oversized furniture, undersized art cars and anything else that sparks their sense of humor and juxtaposes realities.

The Illuminaughty Chakra Tower was a labor of love by 20 friends brought together by the San Francisco Late Night Dance community led by the Towermistress (aka April Minor) in 2001. The camp started off as a tower of naked bodies and gradually evolved into a Chakra Tower. Using a 28-foot tower of scaffolding, the group employed wooden frames and chicken wire to mount a wild artistic sculpture on it.

Jerry James was born in Tripoli, Libya, and grew up in an Air Force family. He dropped out of college in 1975 and by chance wound up in construction. By the time he started building the first Burning Man in 1986, he was experienced in directing construction crews and thrived on completing prototypical projects under challenging conditions. Assembling and then burning a 30-foot pre-fabricated sculpture on a beach with a semi-professional crew and no injuries or arrests was his perfect project. Jerry chose not to continue working with Larry after 1989, citing creative differences. He now lives in Mill Valley and continues his career in custom residential construction.

Justice League Camp was designed and built by engineers and musicians who could never agree on aesthetics, so they settled for the sturdiest thing they could think of. They didn't even know what they had built (a "Quonset hut" structure) until the guy from the next camp told them as he was helping to put it up. The design fed both the egotistical and the group mind. The living area was an open half-shell into which anyone could, and did, drive their own easy chair up and prop their feet on the table as an equal. There was no overriding concept other than to amuse oneself and anyone around. The name "Justice League" was derived from a simple desire to wear pajamas and capes in the desert.

Syd Klinge is an artist-adventurer based in Los Angeles. His varied career has included work as an actor, musician, performance artist, sculptor, film editor, recording studio technician and builder of high-power Tesla coils. During his first year at Burning Man in 1997, he was inspired by both the art and the renegade spirit of the community. In 2000, he designed and built *Hearth*, with friend and collaborator Charlie "Chunks" Smith, and brought it back to the desert in 2001.

Oakland artist **Jay Kravitz** has been pouring energy into the Bay Area art scene since he first cast wild eyes on it in 1991. He now survives as the senior artist at the University of California Office of the President. After first attending Burning Man in 1995, he helped Michael Christian on *Nebulous Entity* in 1998 and *Flock* in 2001, and created his own sculpture in 1999. Jay was also a core driving force behind the *Iron Cupola* project, melting 6,000 pounds of metal into a giant wishbone. Jay's work, encompassing metal, glass, fire, ink, found objects, graphic design, music and performance, twists sculpture into visual and tactile emblems of life.

The first time **Lush** went to Burning Man, eight years ago, they were just a few tree trimmers and a hairdresser. Initially they wanted to create shade structures, a safe haven for family and friends. They always enjoyed the challenges thrown at them by the extreme elements of the desert and as their survival experience grew, so did their creativity. A surfacing submarine, *H.M.S. Love*, a grove of glowing palm trees, a towering Celtic mushroom and a giant desert flower were all a tribute to the inspiration created by Burning Man. The family grows larger with new, creative people contributing what they can.

M. Mara-Ann is a San Francisco based poet and visual artist. Her kinetic poetry sculptures featured at Burning Man include collaborations *Cochlea* (2000), *Duration* (1999) with Travis Ortiz and solo pieces *Chance Sublimation* (1998), and *Terza Preghiera* (1997), with production support from Giamma Clerici. Mara is intrigued by the relativity of scale that sculptural language engages within the vastness of the playa — particularly when given movement.

Dan Macchiarini, aka Danny Mac, started playing with torch fire 42 years ago at age six when his late father, artist Peter, taught him to solder. He makes metal sculpture and jewelry in the studio his father started in 1948 in San Francisco. The *Dragon Smelter*, aka *B.R.C. Dragon 1* and *Kukla the Happy Dragon*, was an idea that grew out of aluminum casting activities at Burning Man 1998 and 1999. During those two years Dan was part of Forge Camp, which led casting events that took the aluminum from cans out of Recycle Camp

and used a small reduction furnace and crucible to melt and pour aluminum into sand molds. In 2000, the Year of the Dragon, Dan created a kinetic dragon sculpture that breathed fire.

Mike McCabe has always been fascinated by fire art; the more interactive, the better. Steel wool, he has found, is a fantastic medium for interactive fire art. Mike has flown a kite with a 20-foot tail of burning steel wool at Burning Man. A flight during a windstorm yielded fiery loop-the-loops and a 200-foot waterfall of sparks.

Mystic Krewe of Satyrs created the *Fire Fantasies of Neptune* for the 1997 Mysteria show, which featured the Shrine of the Mermaid. The group, inspired by the Mistick Krewes that have paraded in New Orleans for Mardi Gras since 1857, creates a float for Burning Man each year. The floats feature blasting torch devices and are led by flambeaux torches, fire breathers and fierce percussion, complete with Mardi Gras throws and beads. The floats were: *Whalagator* (1997), *Le Boeuf Gras D'or* (1998), *Phoenix* (1999), *Drago de Foc* (2000) and *Mothamorphosis* (2001).

Lisa Nigro has been designing elaborate costumes for Burning Man since 1996. In 1999, she built *Diana*, a 12-foot fertility Goddess and working sundial made of steel rod, expanded metal and mud. At night, 13 women danced with fire at her feet. A hot poker to the Goddesses' yoni sparked an explosion of fireworks and excitement — which ultimately gave birth to Lisa's dragon, *Draka*, the following year. Inspired by the description of a dragon clock tower in the book *Wicked*, *Draka* came to life with the assistance of a dozen cowgirls on Hualapai Ranch, 15 miles north of Black Rock Desert. Mobile and spitting fire, *Draka* is built on a Ford Econoline box truck hauling three trailers. Her scales were cut from 55-gallon steel barrels and the belly, made of cedar shingles, served as a bed for her minions. Another segment contained a bar and lounge, and DJs played in the third section.

Since his arrival in San Francisco from Argentina in 1975, **Pepe Ozan** has explored different fields in the visual arts: props for theater, contemporary furniture and costume design, scenery, painting, sculpture and film. Ancient philosophical, religious and aesthetic concepts have inspired and shaped Pepe's productions. Since 1993 he has been writing, directing and producing operas for Burning Man. In 1996, he researched Byzantine history in Istanbul for *The Arrival of Empress Zoe*. In 1997, he spent six months in India and lived with the Brahmins in the temple of Chidambaram for *The Temple of Rudra*. In 1999, he conducted a study in Voodoo religion in Haiti to develop the script for *Le Mystère de Papa Loko*.

Helping make the operas possible were: Christopher Fuelling, performance director; Twan Uljev, Minister of Communications; Eric Oberthaler, composer; Kevin Borroughs, the secret weapon; Professor Rubik, builder; Paradox Pollack, choreographer; and Jim Gasperini, general coordinator; among many others.

In the summer of 1998, **Kiki Pettit** was on a camping trip with friend Leslie Picardo when they discovered the camping stove wouldn't light because the stove's fuel container had been filled with water. They dumped out the stove into a cup, and, having nothing to do and nothing to eat, Leslie lit the cup. It burned down to the level of the water then stopped. "I thought to myself, 'now that's kinda cool!'" Kiki recounts. She did experiments in a bucket in her tub to see if she could maintain a flame on the water by continually injecting fuel at the top of a stream of water. When she succeeded, Kiki built two water fountains on fire, *The Ceramic Thing* and *The Cauldron*, for Burning Man 1999.

New York native **Peri Pfenninger** moved to the Bay Area from Napa Valley and Humboldt County in 1999. Her first Burning Man project was part of the *Wheel of Time*, and consisted of six mixed media sculptures over 12 feet tall, which she created over the course of eight months. She also wrote and directed a large performance for the installation. In 2001, Peri developed and produced the Coliseum for the Seven Ages theme, having both created the majority of the artwork as well as directed other artists. She collaborated with Charlie Peling; Jim Standard, who constructed the structure for the plasma pillar; Robin Silva, who worked on sound; and Clint Kaster, who worked on sound and lighting.

Equal parts social experiment, conceptual art piece and rock solid shelter, **Plug 4** was designed and prefabricated at a dairy farm in central California out of two tons of lumber. It became the 22-foot tall, bright orange, six sided, two-story shrine to one of the simplest man-made achievements that makes Burning Man possible: the extension cord plug. Day-time movie theater, night-time dance floor and full-time home of SOW 4080, the Giant Ghetto Blaster, *Plug 4's* power was unmistakable and unforgettable to those who felt it.

Loosely based on the designs of Buckminster Fuller, the **Pyromid** is a four-sided, latticed, wooden pyramid which rises some 35 feet high and covers nearly 1,200 square feet of playa. It is built from more than 1,000 three-foot pine slats, each one cut from nine-foot lengths and pre-drilled. Assembly is done on the playa with each piece laced and bolted by hand. Due to the structure's size and weight, the crew has devised a unique top-down construction process whereby over the course of three days, the *Pyramid* literally rises from the desert as the builders add a layer, then lift, then add another layer, and so on. On the day after the Man is burned, the *Pyramid* is lifted from its position on the Esplanade and slowly carried to a predetermined sacrificial spot where a crack demolition team packs it with dry wood, pyrotechnics and gallons of flammable liquid and sets it on fire.

David Schlussel has been a citizen of Black Rock City since 1996. In 1997, he built the *Fertility Tiki Gods*, with John Warno, as a part of Camp DominOasis. In 1998, came *The Interterrestrials*, a spiral of mud people climbing out of the ground, and the *Chrome and Copper Couple Copulating*. In 1999, he worked with Jeff Schoonhoven and Annalisa Chasan to build some untitled gravity defying fractured clay and steel figures. In 2000, he created an environmental piece called *Savasana*, a field of wind chimes way out in the playa. John Warno, Gordon McIver, Slater Penny, Sara Mathison, other helper elves, and Camp DominOasis helped make the Tiki Gods.

Dave Siegel, aka Danger Dave, is a commercial photographer who moved from Southern California to Reno in 1994 to be closer to the freedom and beauty of the Nevada desert. The following year he discovered Burning Man and found himself at home. When he's not in the studio, Dave is a master of mechanical mayhem and can often be found out on the playa or working at a local opal mine in the Black Rock mountains. In 2001, he brought his *Brain Mobile* (aka *Your Brain on Playa*). The art car has a big smile and blue eyes of electroluminescent wire and a pulsing, luminescent brain fixed to a golf cart.

Charlie Smith, a sculptor and maker of art furniture, has a degree in painting and experimental media. Charlie, who lives in Atlanta, Georgia, created *Fire Bike* in 1998. He built the *Hearth* in 2000 and 2001 in collaboration with Syd Heartha and *Infanity* in 2001 in collaboration with Syd, Meagan Clark and Kathlene Turner.

Kimric Smythe first attended Burning Man in 1991. From 1992 to 2000, he and Scott Fickus, with help from Kimric's father Bill, created the pyrotechnics on the Man himself. He also helped start the LampLighters with Steve Mobia, The Driveby Shooting range; the Java Cow; the *Clock Tower*; small flame cannons and kite-mounted fireworks. He re-engineered the burning of the Man in the mid-1990s, using wax instead of diesel, increasing the weight of fuel from 50 lbs.

to 250 lbs. so the Man no longer had to be lowered just before the burn. He also came up with the idea of dancing down the Man using the guy cables in 1997.

Sunbrothers **Kevin Gauna** and **Dennis Baum** began growing solar-powered plant sculptures in 1995. Since 1998, they've been transplanting whole gardens in the playa for Burning Man. Every year the brothers, residents at Camp Carp, try to out-do themselves, growing a more ambitious garden than the last, ranging from sunflowers and pea vines to roses and corn stalks. The plants are made of copper branches and leaves, the flowers and fruit are hand-blown glass and solar panels are embedded in the leaves. During the day the solar panels charge the plant up, and at night the flowers glow, fade, and change color.

Landscape designer **Don Syrek** first attended Burning Man in 1997. With help from his friends in Tic Toc Town, including Valerie Syrek, Loren and Rachel Carpenter and Randy Behymer, he created the *Time Tunnel* in 1999. The 80-foot by 40-foot time machine had thousands of computer-controlled sequencing rainbow lights that zipped back and forth to create the illusion of movement in the tunnel. At one end was a primordial burning volcano representing the beginning of time. Looking through the tunnel in the distance was the Man, representing the end of time. Don often traveled throughout the Playa, in his *Flying Saucer* art car, abducting innocent bystanders and transporting them through the tunnel.

Michael Taluc has been pitting his large-scale wood, steel and fabric sculptures against the forces of the playa since 1995. Since the destruction of his first playa piece by gale-force winds eight years ago, his work has endeavored to find a symbiosis with the powerful conditions present in the desert. The vertical and red nature of recent pieces take great advantage of their contrast to the flat, monochromatic venue at Burning Man. When not on the playa, Michael can be found in Portland, Ore.

John Warno was born and raised in Long Beach, Calif. He first experienced Burning Man in 1996 where he met David Schlussel. The two returned to the desert in 1997 to co-create the *Fertility Tikis*, John's first large-scale sculpture. At Burning Man 2000, John erected a mixed media sculpture called *The Babel Project*, a 23-foot high circular metal tower covered in over 120 plaster life casts of female torsos. Light beamed from within the tower while the sound of female voices undulated from a single voice to a montage of

women speaking different languages. Renee Ting, sound designer, contributed invaluable expertise, as did David Schlussel, Jelena Ristic, Jeff Schoonhoven, Jason Meyer, Gordon McIver, Vivian Dwyer, Jen Alison, Eli Novin, Brian Sherman, Frog Gilmore and all the models.

Russell Wilcox is a Bay Area artist and laser engineer who has attended Burning Man since 1996. His first project was a solar-powered electric car. Beginning in 1999, he built three laser installations on the playa: *The Tetrahedron* (1999), *Beaming Man* (2000), and *The Grid* (2001). These were large-scale geometric environments (from 20 feet to 4,000 feet across) made of stationary laser beams. The last two projects required a team of professionals to build the custom laser hardware, including Ernest Bennett (metalwork) and Greg Kiskaden (electronics). Russell has worked on the world's largest laser systems at the Lawrence Livermore Laboratory, but finds the harsh environment of Black Rock City a special challenge.

Aaron Wolf Baum, aka Doctor Friendly, is a National Science Foundation Fellow who studied physics at Harvard and Stanford University, where he received a Ph.D. in 1997. His work with fractal and living system-inspired electronic music began the same year. His first major project was a system that used fractals to continuously process and layer audio samples obtained from popular culture and the local environment via microphones. This system formed the voice of the *Nebulous Entity*, a giant, roving alien information scavenger that serenaded thousands of people at Burning Man 1998. His next project was to develop an audio texture generator to make weeks of environmental organic-electronic music without human intervention. This project was exhibited in numerous galleries, audio/video shows and multimedia conferences in the Bay Area.

Michael Zelner and **Suki O'Kane** are the creators of the *Time Chime*, installed at Burning Man in 1999. The piece was a freestanding, monumental wind chime that suspended twelve tuned pipes from the top of a 20-foot high wood frame. Arranged as a clock face, the pipes were sounded by a wooden clapper with a long tendril and padded seat attached. Participants sat on the seat, one at a time, drifting the clapper among the pipes to sound the chimes. When *Time Chime* was unattended, it sounded in response to the wind. The chime tones were intended to be subtle, multi-layered and resonant. The artists have been commissioned to re-create the *Time Chime* for permanent installation in a community art space in San Francisco.

Elinor Mills Abreu hasn't seen anything as wild as Burning Man since her days as a toddler in Haight Ashbury. When not exploring the aesthetics of adult playgrounds, Elinor writes about cyberspace security, privacy and other cutting-edge technology issues for Reuters in San Francisco.

Rob Brezsny writes *Free Will Astrology*, an internationally syndicated weekly column that reaches nine million readers in 132 publications and the web at www.freewill-astrology.com. When *Utne Reader* named him a "Culture Hero," it observed, "With a blend of spontaneous poetry, feisty politics, and fanciful put-on, Brezsny breathes new life into the tabloid mummy of zodiac advice columns." His book, *The Televisionary Oracle*, inspired novelist Tom Robbins to say, "I've seen the future of American literature and its name is Rob Brezsny."

Jennifer C. Clemente returned to her native west coast after spending the 90's reporting on Eastern and Central Europe's socio-political transition and living the bohemian expatriate dream. Jennifer, aka Kakao Chouva, participates in diverse community experiments in the Bay Area and spins eclectic beats as DJ Chaka.

Brittany Corrigan was raised in Colorado and graduated from Reed College in Portland, Ore. Her poems have appeared in *The Texas Observer, Hayden's Ferry Review, Borderlands: Texas Poetry Review, The Blue Mesa Review, Stringtown* and *Many Mountain Moving*. She works for a small publishing company in Portland.

Shannon Coulter is a writer and researcher. Ten years of San Francisco life have not diminished her longing for autumn in the Northeast. She first attended Burning Man in 2001 and purchased her 2002 ticket the first week they went on sale.

Sadie Damascus is short, loud and lives on the Russian River. She is a Vermonter, a grandmother, a writer, an educator, a comedian, a mystic, an artist, an instigator and a traditional folksinger. She holds a Doctorate of Bovinity from Bovine University. For the past seven years she has been online, attending Burning Man and married to woodcarver Grover Damascus.

d6 has been creatively misguided since the age of nine, finding solace in all aspects of creative effort. He personally focuses on sound, and has promoted underground shows of all kinds since 1989. d6 is dedicated to Maisie, Sophie, Lynn and The Man.

Dave Eggers is the editor of McSweeney's, and has written two books, including the New York Times bestseller *A Heartbreaking Work of Staggering Genius*. He lives in San Francisco.

William L. Fox has published 14 collections of poetry and six non-fiction books about cognition and landscape. He has had fellowships recently from the National Science Foundation, the Getty Research Institute, the Lannan Foundation and the Guggenheim Foundation.

Anne L. Francis is a writer and painter living in San Francisco. She attended Burning Man for the first time in 2000.

Larry Harvey is executive director of the Burning Man Project, serves as chairman of its senior staff and Black Rock City LLC, its executive committee. He also co-chairs the organization's Art Department, scripts and co-curates Burning Man's annual art theme and collaborates with artists in creating aspects of the art theme and the design of Black Rock City. He has, by his own admission, a grandiose imagination. This is tempered by a love of people and a keen appreciation of their characters, capacities and creative ideas.

Helen13, is a writer and photographer. In the days of punk, ska, new wave and goth she ran the establishments Retail Slut, Wild Planet and the fanzine *Foetus Acid*. Then the energy waned, house, trance and jungle filled the dance floors and Helen filled the pages of *Lotus* magazine, Grooveradio.com and *hE@D* magazine. From Ibiza to Temecula she goes to immerse in the new, the next, the nirvana.

Reed Hortie is a humorist living in Vancouver, Canada. His writing runs the gamut from children's plays to stand-up comedy. Reed is currently working on his cabaret show "The Hairy Palms Apartment/Hotel," a musical romp through the wacky world of self-abuse.

Tom Kramer is a Bay Area native with a passion for creativity and life philosophy. His outlets include poetry, photography, improv and high-tech marketing. He founded the Urban Iditarod in 1994 and first went to Burning Man in 1992.

Jay Kravitz has been placing pen to paper for the better part of his life, delicately sculpting and molding to deliver the inner beauty inherent in each word. He has worked in many capacities including poetry, fiction, grant writing and graffiti — none of which have delivered him into a life of riches and fame.

Michael Magoski has been a poet and photographer for 20 years. Working out of his studio/gallery in southern California, the Violet Hour, Michael and wife Candace, costume design, couture and make-up artist, specialize in exotic environmental portraiture using infrared films and alternative photographic processes including Polaroid transfer.

Rita Manachi fled the Middle East with her mother and younger brother in 1979. She now lives in the Bay Area.

M. Mara-Ann is a San Francisco based poet, visual artist, and publisher of the online journal *WOOD: dialogues among poetry and the visual arts*. Her new book *lighthouse* (2002) was just released by Atelos. Mara strives to liberate poetic language from fear of difficulty, and believes all language as sound belongs to us — emerging from us as we emerge from it.

Sean McKnight has been an artist most of his life in such areas as music, experimental video production, photography, writing and fire performances. As such, he was drawn to his first Burning Man pilgrimage in 2001. Sean is currently a multimedia/graphic design instructor at three different colleges in the Northeast.

Ron Meiners is a poet and painter, and creator of online community. He volunteers with the Burning Man Media Team and with the Black Rock Arts Foundation.

Clear Menser is an artist. He lives in South Pasadena.

Andy Moore has been a fixer of things for the past 9 years. Currently he is an engineering student who likes to work for the Black Rock City Department of Public Works, and lives stealthily in the Northwest while surviving on microbrews.

Eilish Nagle is a practitioner of verbal, visual and healing arts in Oakland, Calif. She has worked as an editor, apple picker, teacher, and ice-cream maker. She is currently working on a collection of poetry.

Vicki Olds, aka shibumi, is a writer, artist, philosopher and creative communications designer and producer. Her volunteer work for Burning Man has included editing and publishing the *Black Rock Gazette*. In 1998, she designed and produced the gallery exhibition *The Art of Burning Man*, staged in all three major public art spaces in San Francisco's Civic Center.

Travis Ortiz is a writer and visual artist living in San Francisco. He has been published in several experimental poetry magazines including *Poetics Journal, Chain, Salt, Mirage #/Period(ical)* and the online journal *WOOD*. He is the author of *geography of parts*. Along with Lyn Hejinian, he is the co-editor and project director of Atelos Publishing Project and is also the founder and editor of the press, *ghos-ti-*. He is dedicated to poetry that challenges inherent notions of what poetry is.

Michael Parsons has been a journalist for longer than he cares to remember, and spent the last six years in San Francisco covering the rise and fall of the Net for *The Industry Standard*. He is currently recovering in London.

R.A. Robertson lives in Austin, Texas where he teaches aikido for a living. He has worked in the computer industry, played in the local music scene and driven a bus. He holds a B.A. in Anthropology from the University of Texas, and enjoys envisioning alternative living strategies, such as supporting the local polyamory community. He recently was seen chasing fairies in Pease Park with a large butterfly net. He caught a few, but let them all go after tagging them for future studies.

Jon Ross is a purveyor of subtle paranoia, bleak intensity and intense non-specific abstraction. Hailing from Great Britain, Jon escaped in the early '90s to dive, camera-first, into the madness of California and the American West. Documenting the surreal landscapes and festivities that prevail there, his photography depicts the Earth and its inhabitants at their most unearthly and insane.

Michael Rothenberg is a poet, novelist, and songwriter. His books of poems include *Favorite Songs, The Paris Journals* and *Unhurried Vision*. He is the author of the novel *Punk Rockwell*. He is also editor of the Internet magazine BigBridge.org, and most recently editor of *As Ever, Selected Poems* by Joanne Kyger (Penguin Books).

Bonnieblaze Schneider has been a poet for over 15 years, publishing two collections of poetry and numerous individual poems. Rumi, Gibran and Pound keep her grounded while skydiving and Burning Man give her flight. A graduate of the New College of California's poetics program, she currently runs naked through San Diego avenues.

Chris Taylor, an itinerant Englishman, is the San Francisco bureau chief of *Time Magazine*. He wanted to be a writer when he was six years old, and still plans to be one when he grows up. Currently he is working on three weblogs: Dailyblah.com, FutureDaze.com and Newtopianews.net.

Daniel Terdiman has been a journalist for seven years, and has worked as a reporter for the451.com and stringer for *Time Magazine* in San Francisco. He has written extensively about technology and business, but now hopes to focus more on social and cultural issues with a technological bent.

Michael Tscheu, LCSW, MBA, is a social worker and health administrator. Most of his career has been devoted to care of the dying and ethical issues. He helped to start hospice care in Sacramento and later helped develop special programs for bereaved children. He is currently the director of a treatment foster care program in Sacramento. Michael has been a contributing artist at Burning Man for the last five years.

Mark Van Proyen is associate professor of art history, painting and digital media at the San Francisco Art Institute. He contributes regularly to *Artweek, The New Art Examiner, Art Issues* and *Art in America*.

Mark Jan Wlodarkiewicz, aka Vordo, edits and designs music and sound for feature and independent films. He is also an eclectic DJ and proprietor of the *abstrakt zone* (abstrakt-zone.com.). His first Burning Man was in 1994 and he is one of the founders of the Spiral Oasis, Burning Man's longest running theme camp.

Allison Yates was trained in the performing arts, but accidentally got a job at HotWired, the online component of *Wired* magazine. There she held various positions, including writing "Ask Allison," one of the Web's first advice columns. After six years in the dot-com world, she is now a certified massage therapist.

Holly Kreuter grew up in Wisconsin, moved to California in 1991, and knew she was home the moment she first stepped foot on the Black Rock Playa in 1995. She successfully stayed as far away as possible from the event organizers for two years before joining the Burning Man team in 1997. She is a senior staff member and, along with Harley Dubois, Theme Camp Coordinatrix. When not creating neighborhoods, you can often find her with a tripod shooting photographs of Burning Man at night. Holly has been patiently collecting Burning Man images and sound for four years.

Elinor Mills Abreu served as prose editorial director for the book. She received a masters degree in journalism and then got her real education in the trenches of the Associated Press, *The Industry Standard* and Reuters. Elinor has been writing and editing news for more than a decade, most of it during the rise and fall of the dotcom revolution. A San Francisco resident, she has been both participant and spectator at Burning Man for six years.

Sean Abreu, a musician, composer and electronic artist of various media, composed all the music for the *Drama in the Desert* companion DVD and did the mastering and sound design. Sean has created scores for independent feature films, including *My Sweet Killer*. Under the name Databass, he recently released a CD titled *Fluid* And a 12-inch record featuring the single "All the Way to Dawn."

Michael Blacksburg brought his experience as legal consultant for Broderbund Software to the project. A recent transplant from New York, Michael has yet to experience Burning Man in all its glory.

Jason Carswell (aka Sunshine) has attended Burning Man since 1999 and Burning Flipside since 2000, but has been freakin' all his life. Raised primarily in British Columbia, Ontario, with stints in Vancouver, Toronto, Manhattan and now San Francisco, he has been directing since 1991 and doing high-end 3-D character animation since 1995. A designer, illustrator and painter since before he can remember, Jason is currently exploring furniture design and has found that music moves him like nothing else can.

Justin Dossetti, an independent filmmaker, did video editing on the *Drama in the Desert* DVD. His work has included the feature film *My Sweet Killer*, Hollywood Video's number one independent rental in 2000. The film won an award at the Method Film Festival and had a theatrical run in Los Angeles. He is also co-founder of The MPFactory Ltd. film production company.

Jason Fisher is a software architect who brought his organizational and planning skills to the *Drama in the Desert* team as the project planner. He has attended Burning Man since 1999, and has experienced some of the most profound moments of his life while on the playa. Among his achievements has been helping to form the Love Rangers theme camp (nomadically supplying your love and attention needs since 2001).

Anne L. Francis, an experienced Web site developer and editor, produced the *Drama in the Desert* website (desertdrama.com) and was its Web mistress in 2001. She was also copy editor for the book. Anne attended Burning Man for the first time in 2000.

Stewart Harris, photographer, visual and audio artist, worked on image production and video editing for the DVD. Weaving in and around the Burning Man scene since back in the day, Stewart participated in the event from 1992 to 1995 and returned in 2000, missing 2001 due to nuptial bliss with font maven Lisa Hoffman. Stewart's photographs were featured on the cover of Databass' *Fluid* CD.

Lisa Hoffman, photographer, sculptor and graphic artist, was the designer of the *Drama in the Desert* book. She is a freelance designer, working on everything from websites to textiles to lifestyles. Lisa is cofounder of Studio Nine Design, an instructor for various computer graphic courses and department coordinator for the Graphic Design department at The Fashion Institute of Design & Merchandising. She participated in Burning Man from 1991 to 1995, returned to the Playa in 2000 and has been map designer for Black Rock City since 2001.

Paul King is helping the team with its business strategy. In 1995, Paul founded and ran Infoscape, a venture funded software company. These days he helps companies with product planning and marketing. He also helped start the Black Rock Arts Foundation. Paul attended Burning Man for the first time in 1997 and has been a huge fan ever since. His interests include neuroscience, video editing, the evolution of cultural patterns and figuring out the nature of reality.

Bruna Lamy was the DVD log-and-capture mistress of video footage and editor of the video interviews. A native of southern California, she is also a visual and digital artist, ceramicist, printmaker, dancer and world citizen. While on the playa in 2001, she volunteered for the Department of Mutant Vehicles.

Michael Lazar is the producer for the companion DVD. He is a recovering software engineer whose long-term creative passions include diving and underwater videography. His work has been sold as stock for nature specials and incorporated into his own video collages orchestrated to electronica music. Most recently he has been focusing on live video performance at clubs and parties. After completing the production of the DVD for *Drama in the Desert*, he intends to continue working as a video producer and composer.

Candace Locklear (aka Evil Pippi) has been a media relations maven for consumer technology companies since moving to San Francisco in early 1996, straight from the redneck riviera of Myrtle Beach, South Carolina. Candace has volunteered for Burning Man since 1997 as its primary media manager. She helped form its 70-person worldwide media team. Currently, Candace serves as a PR consultant for Openwave Systems Inc. and is the publicity manager for *Drama in the Desert*.

M. Mara-Ann is a San Francisco based poet, visual artist, and publisher of experimental poetry. Her online journal *WOOD* features collaborations between poets and visual artists exploring the boundaries and relationships between written and visual mediums. Mara's new book *lighthouse* (2002) was just released by Atelos, while other work includes the chapbook *forthcoming: ecnelis* (2000) from a+bend press and a CD poetry/music collaboration with composer Sean Abreu entitled *Water Rights* (2000). She has attended Burning Man since 1993 and built kinetic poetry sculptures on the playa since 1997. Mara is a poetry editor for *Drama in the Desert*.

Nicole Maron is a freelance information architect and interaction designer in San Francisco who has worked on the Burning Man tech team since January 2001. She is fascinated by all aspects of Human-Computer Interaction (HCI) and is participating in the interaction design and general catherding of the *Drama in the Desert* DVD. She first attended Burning Man in 1998.

Dave Marr first heard of Burning Man in 1996. After attending the event in 1998, he knew he'd found a place to call home and promptly moved to San Francisco to be closer to the Burning Man Project. In late 1999, he began volunteering his web and design skills to Burningman.com. Currently he is the WebTeam Lead for Burning Man's official website and in December 2001 he assumed the role of webmaster for the *Drama in the Desert* website.

Karen McGrath has spent the past eight years professionally as a business consultant, entrepreneur and manager of many flavors, after dabbling in mathematics in Berkeley and juggling numbers around the Bay Area. Karen is financial advisor for Raised Barn Press, also contributing expertise in business strategy and product marketing. Her best work is usually done while playing with her camera or plying her friends with floral and culinary treats. Karen first danced on the playa in 1995 and continues to visit Black Rock City frequently.

Travis Ortiz is a writer and visual artist living in San Francisco. He has been published in several experimental poetry magazines and is the author of a book of poetry entitled *geography of parts*. He is the co-editor and project director of Atelos, a project which publishes authors who push or dismantle the boundaries of poetry. Travis is the founder and editor of the press, *ghos-ti-*, dedicated to publishing poetry that highlights the visual aspects of language. Travis began attending Burning Man in 1999 and has received a grant from Burning Man to create an installation on the Playa for 2002 entitled *Linguistic Islands*. He edited poetry and produced graphics for *Drama in the Desert*.

Ian Rhett is a brainstorm in a bucket of love. He is a communications strategist, founder of the Children's Philanthropy Foundation, and a two-time business owner and entrepreneur. Ian is a business advisor to the project. He attended Burning Man for the first time in 2000.

Dave Skaff is a director, writer and producer of film, video and animation. He helped to produce and direct the DVD companion to the book. Like most Burners, his ideas exceed his available hours. He has spent the majority of the past three Burning Men beginning sentences by saying "Man, next year I'm gonna ..."

Chris Taylor is San Francisco bureau chief for *Time Magazine* and writes mostly about technology. He has been experiencing Burning Man since 1999. An unabashed stylist and ruthless whittler, Chris helped *Drama in the Desert* find its true voice.

Daniel Terdiman is a member of the Burning Man class of 1998. He has written for the *Black Rock Gazette*, created and hosted 2000's Attention Camp, and is a current member of the Burning Man media team. Daniel, a prose editor on the book, is a staff writer for online technology journal *the451*.

Colophon

This book and DVD are yours now: documents that will continue to live and breathe with each examination. As its proud parents, though, we would like to present you with a few of its vital statistics from first idea to final reality.

Number of weeks to produce the book: 63
Photographs in Holly's collection considered for the project: 560
Photographs in book: 286
Fonts used: Legacy Serif for essays, Legacy Serif for poems, Niederwald for title and page numbers
Number of meetings: 88
Most meetings in one month: 16
Types of food consumed during meetings: 23
Meetings with book industry professionals to learn the business: 9
Total contributors and collaborators: 90
Total number of years the production team has attended Burning Man: 93
Number of nicknames given to team members during project: 4
Age range of core team: 26 to 45
Male to female ratio: 15 to 9
Astrological signs represented among the core team: 10
Most team members in one sign: 4
Ratio of air to fire to water to earth signs: 3:7:8:5
Weddings among team members: 2
Number of computers used for the project: 28
Ratio of Macs to PCs: 19 to 9
Gigabytes of hard drive space devoted entirely to the project: 1096
Typos in book: 1

Glossary

Ancestors — The fire dust devils produced by the burn in 2001

Annapurna — One of the Himalaya Mountains in north-central Nepal

Art — Life

Bilocate — Being in two places at one time; a technique used by Danger Ranger

Black Rock City — Home

Black Rock Mobile Library — Roving book-mobile on the Playa

BLM — Bureau of Land Management

BM — Burning Man

BRC — Black Rock City

Burn Platform — DPW-issue corrugated steel structure designed to reduce burn scarring on the desert surface

Butoh — A dance form developed in postwar Japan which rejects Eastern and Western dance convention

Cacophony Society — Merry pranksters who spit in the face of definition

Car-B-Q — An automobile shell fire pit made by Camp Skynrd of Gigsville

The Cage — Workspace in Los Angeles for the Dragon Debris group

Coelacanth — Prehistoric fishes of the order Coelacanthiformes, previously thought to be extinct

Critical Tits — Annual all women's topless bike ride modeled after the Critical Mass bicycle rides in the Bay Area

DPW — The Department of Public Works, builders of Black Rock City infrastructure

Earth Guardians — Volunteers involved in the year-round conservation of the Black Rock Playa

E.L. Wire — Electro Luminescent wire, a nontoxic, flexible tube containing phosphor

Esplanade — The main drag of Black Rock City

Fuckos — Citizens of Gigsville

Geodesic Dome — A popular playa shelter design; originally developed by R. Buckminster Fuller

Guy Lines — Rope, wire or cable used to tie down and support structures against wind

Gypsum — Highly alkaline mineral consisting of hydrous calcium sulfate that comprises most of the Black Rock Desert

Hualapai — Small desert playa located near Black Rock

LED — Light-emitting diode

Life — Art

LNT — Leave No Trace; the core environmental philosophy of Black Rock citizens

Mad Max — Post-apocalyptic gothic anti-hero

Mandala — Graphic symbol of the universe depicted in geometric patterns

Moop — Matter-Out-Of-Place; reference to litter

Obtainium — Found items available for the taking

Playa — Dry lakebed

Poi — chain, cable, rope or string with a fire wick, ball or flag attached to the end and used for dancing

Port-a-Potty — Repository of human excremental deposits

Promenade — Central path from Center Camp Café to the Man

Radio Free Burning Man — One of the pirate radio stations on the playa

Rebar — Steel rod with ridges used for staking and reinforcing structures; main cause of injuries on the playa

Rigid Pickle — That which stands at attention

RV — Recreational Vehicle

Seven Ages — 2000 Burning Man Theme; based on the Seven Ages of Man soliloquy in Shakespeare's "As You Like It"

Tesla — High-voltage art experience

Theme Camp — Camp created by participants that is interactive and civic in nature

Trego Hot Springs — One of the many hot springs ringing the Black Rock Desert

Turd Burglar — Mythical creatures who clean the Porta-Potties

White Out — Dust storm resulting in zero visibility

The First Burning Man

Photographed by Jerry James © 1986

Production Credits

Still Photographer, Producer
Holly Kreuter

Book Design/ Cover Design
Lisa Hoffman

Prose Editorial Team
Elinor Mills Abreu
Chris Taylor
Daniel Terdiman

Poetry Editorial Team
M. Mara-Ann
Travis Ortiz

Copy Editor
Anne L. Francis

Image Preparation
Jason Carswell
Justin Dossetti
Stewart Harris
Lisa Hoffman
Travis Ortiz

Writing Contributors
Elinor Mills Abreu
Rob Brezsny
Jennifer C. Clemente
Brittney (Lola) Corrigan
Shannon Coulter
d6
Sadie Damascus
Dave Eggers
William L. Fox
Anne L. Francis
Katrina Glerum
Larry Harvey
helen13
Reed Hortie
John Kelly
Tom Kramer
Jay Kravitz
Michael Magoski
Rita Manachi
M. Mara-Ann
Ian McFarland

Sean McNight
Ron Meiners
Clear Menser
Andrew Moore
Eilish Nagle
Vicki Olds
Travis Ortiz
Michael Parsons
Tony Perez
R.A. Robertson
Jon Ross
Michael Rothenberg
Bonnie Schneider
Chris Taylor
Daniel Terdiman
Michael Tscheu
Mark Van Proyen
Alex Wilson
Mark Jan Wlodarkiewicz
Allison Yates

Photo Contribution
Jerry James
Gabe Kirchheimer

Webmaster
Anne L. Francis
Dave Marr

Legal Counsel
Michael Blacksburg

Business Team
Michael Blacksburg
Paul King
Candace Locklear
Karen McGrath
Ian Rhett

Project Planner
Jason Fisher

DVD Menu Architecture
Michael Lazar
Nicole Maron

DVD Authoring
Michael Lazar

DVD Interface Design
Michael Lazar

Original Music
Sean Abreu

Playa Sounds Recorded by
Stewart Harris
Holly Kreuter

Video Editors
Stewart Harris — Day 1
Jason Carswell — Days 2 & 5
Justin Dossetti — Days 3 & 4
Dave Skaff — Day 6
Josh Hittleman — Day 7

Video Log and Capture/Librarian
Bruna Lamy

Interview Editing
Jason Carswell
Bruna Lamy

Video Interviews Conducted by
Holly Kreuter
Bruna Lamy

Video Contributors
Elinor Mills Abreu
Sean Abreu
Peter Baily
Gary Brown
Timothy Childs
Dan Doerner
Josh Hittleman
Bruna Lamy
Chris Ralph
Brian Scully
Dave Skaff
Sigi Torinus

Creative Consultant
Lisa Hoffman

Special Thanks to

Black Rock City LLC, Burning Man Staff and Volunteers, Argyre Patras, Bill Brownstein, Brian Behlendorf, Bob Wallace, Carson Kelly, Cate Reigner, Dave Eggers, Denise Garbinski, Exploring Music, FIDM, Gabe Kirchheimer, Isabella La Rocca, Jennifer Morgano, Jerry James, Jim Home, Jon Drukman, Larry Harvey, Kathleen Craig, KathyAnne Woodruff, Marcy Swenson, Mark Van Proyen, Medusa, Nancy Ballard, Peter Freund, P-Ter Normal, Rod Garrett, all of our parents and the citizens of Black Rock City — without you, the DPW would have nothing to complain about and could sit around all day and night drinking beer and shooting guns and blowing stuff up, and come to think of it that wouldn't be all bad, and maybe next year ...